"Everybody needs a book that can help them through their workday and provide ongoing guidance and support. *What Would Buddha Do at Work?* is truly a comforting companion. If I were a manager, I would throw out the company policy manual and use *What Would Buddha Do at Work?* instead."

Mark Bryan,
co-author of *The Artist's Way at Work: Riding the Dragon*

"Every day you spend in making a living is a chance to find personal fulfillment and, even more to the point, Enlightenment. Awakening comes from something you do, not something you are. This very useful book can awaken you to the possibilities your workplace has to offer—it can help you make a living and a life."

Rev. Kusala, Bhikshu, Buddhist monk,
International Buddhist Meditation Center, Los Angeles

"The Zen teacher Suzuki said that Buddhism can be summed up in two words: 'Not always so.' Metcalf and Gallagher take the same playful approach in *WWBD@W*—a book rich in wisdom, practical in orientation, and ever so relevant to work. This is a book you will enjoy again and again, an invitation to inner creativity and outward focus."

Alan Briskin, author of *The Stirring of Soul in the Workplace*
and co-author of *Bringing Your Soul to Work: An Everyday Practice*

"As a physician, manager, and teacher of seminars, I interact with people on every level. In reading *WWBD@W*, I agreed not only with much of Buddha's wisdom as it has evolved through the ages, but also with how it applies to situations we all encounter in today's workplace. BJ and Franz have done a superb job of integrating Buddhist concepts with work life issues."

Arnold Chanin, M.D.
Medical Director
Centinela/El Segundo Medical Center

"*WWBD@W* is practical Buddhism—enlightened concepts brought down to everyday reality. What could be more useful?"

Jay Roewe, Vice President of Production, HBO Films

What Would Buddha Do at Work?

101 Answers to Workplace Dilemmas

Franz Metcalf & BJ Gallagher Hateley

Foreword by Ken Blanchard

Seastone

BERKELEY, CALIFORNIA

BERRETT-KOEHLER PUBLISHERS, INC.
San Francisco

Published by:
Seastone, an imprint of Ulysses Press
P.O. Box 3440
Berkeley, CA 94703
www.ulyssespress.com

and

Berrett-Koehler Publishers, Inc.
450 Sansome Street, Suite 1200
San Francisco, CA 94111
www.bkconnection.com

ISBN: 1-56975-300-8

Printed in the USA by R. R. Donnelley & Sons

10 9 8 7 6 5 4 3 2 1

Library of Congress Cataloging-in-Publication Data

Metcalf, Franz Aubrey.
    What would Buddha do at work? : 101 answers to workplace dilemmas /
  Franz Metcalf & BJ Gallagher Hateley.
     p. cm.
    Includes bibliographical references.
    ISBN 1-56975-300-8 (alk. paper)
    1. Business. 2. Religious life--Buddhism. 3. Interpersonal relations--Religious
aspects--Buddhism. I. Hateley, BJ Gallagher. II. Title.
    BQ5400.M48 2001
    294.3'44--dc21   00-065727

Editor: Steven Zah Schwartz
Editorial and production staff: Claire Chun, Lily Chou, Marin Van Young
Design: Leslie Henriques, Sarah Levin
Cover photograph: Robert Holmes

The publishers have generously given permission to use quotations from the works cited on page 171.

Distributed in the United States by Publishers Group West. For all other countries contact Berrett-Koehler Publishers, Inc., at 415-288-0260.

We dedicate this book to all workers throughout space and time,
to those who work to live and those who live to work.
May Buddha's words and wisdom reach your eyes,
awaken your minds, and guide your feet along the path.

Acknowledgments

The fruits of this collaboration have been sweet and bountiful. We know this because *WWBD@W* is the collaboration not only of two authors, but of two publishers, and would be unthinkable without all of us. Together, we have savored the fruits of creativity, spirituality, mutual learning, new perspectives, and new friendships. For these we are deeply grateful.

We want to thank Ray Riegert and Leslie Henriques for the original idea of *WWBD*, Steven Schwartz for his gentle and thorough editorial guidance, Bryce Willett for his marketing moxie, and Claire Chun and all the other good people at Ulysses who brought this book to fruition. We also wish to thank our kindred spirits at Berrett-Koehler: Steve Piersanti for pushing us with his hard questions, Jeevan Sivasubramaniam for his unflagging support, and Pat Anderson, whose superb partnering instincts led her to pair BJ with Franz (the Peacock meets the Buddha). And we thank Publishers Group West for their early input, suggesting Buddha's insights be focused on the world of work. Thank you one and all. We bow to you.

Individually, we bow to our families and loved ones, the people who support and encourage us: Nina Ruscio; and Gloria, Ken, and Karen Gallagher.

Finally, we bow to Buddha for his profound insight and wisdom, and for his dedication in opening the path for us and for the world.

Table of Contents

Part II: Cultivating Enlightened Work Relationships   55

Foreword

by Ken Blanchard

Does Buddha have anything to offer non-Buddhists in the workplace? My answer is a wholehearted, enthusiastic "Yes." Let me explain why.

As Chief Spiritual Officer of The Ken Blanchard Companies, every morning I leave a global voicemail message to inspire our people to be their best and to remember our mission and values. This message is then posted on our intranet and made available to all the two hundred and eighty Blanchard Associates in the U.S., Canada, and Great Britain. Why do we go to this much trouble? Because I believe that deep down in all of us is a little voice that cries out "Inspire me! Help me be the kind of person I want to be."

As a follower of Jesus, I believe He is the truth and the way. So I look for my inspiration from Him as documented in the Bible. And yet, in our company we have people of all faiths as well as people who center their faith in the goodness of human beings. The Golden Rule is their mantra. As a result, many of our people would delete my morning messages if they thought I was only coming from a Christian perspective. So I look for inspirational messages from a variety of sources besides Jesus. Our folks get to hear words of wisdom from great prophets and spiritual leaders like Buddha, Mohammed, Moses, Mahatma Gandhi, Yogananda, and the Dalai Lama, as well as inspirational lay leaders like Nelson Mandela, Martin Luther King, and Dag Hammarskjöld. The wonderful thing is that this variety doesn't weaken the messages—it strengthens them, because all of these leaders share one profound conviction: true happiness comes only when the center of the universe is not yourself. Like Jesus, they lead the refrain of kindness, compassion, forgiveness, honesty, hard work, patience, loyalty, and peace.

As a Christian, I learned things from this book that I had not known before, since I had not previously done any extensive exploration of Eastern philosophies and religions. I learned that Buddha was not a god or a messiah, he was a wise teacher and a psychologist. He did not tell people to worship him; he invited people to follow his example and pursue enlightenment. He pointed to the path, but he was not the path. In fact, he was concerned when people wanted to worship him, because it is easier for people to worship him than follow him.

I loved reading *WWBD@W*. It made me think; it made me chuckle; it made me reflect on how I participate in leading our human resource development organization, and how I advise my clients on their organizations. This little book is like having Buddha as one of your mentors or coaches—someone who can help you with real-world problems. This book does not tell you to retreat from the world to meditate on some mountaintop (although Buddhist meditation is helpful for staying centered in a stressful world). This book tells you how to engage in action, how to live the principles of compassion, right livelihood, and mindfulness, being fully present in each moment.

This book is rich with words of wisdom for people in organizations both large and small—for employees as well as supervisors, managers, and executives. Its teachings about dealing with change are especially helpful. Through this book, Buddha's insights and words help us create a kinder and gentler workplace. Jesus would approve . . . and so would Moses, Mohammed, and other great prophets and spiritual leaders. And so do I. This is wisdom for the whole world.

Buddha points to the path and invites us to begin our journey to enlightenment. I point to this little jewel of a book and invite you to begin (or continue) your journey to enlightened work.

K. B.

Introduction

Putting Buddha to Work

This book is for people who seek to benefit from ancient spiritual wisdom by applying it to their current workplace problems and situations. Does this mean ancient solutions to today's problems? In some cases, yes. But this also means new perspectives on timeless troubles. As you get into this book, you'll see what we mean.

Most people who perform paid work outside the home spend more of their waking time at work than anywhere else. They see their bosses more than they do their spouses. They spend more time and energy dealing with difficult coworkers than they do with their own difficult children. For many, work itself has become an important way to establish personal identity, to meet social needs, to build satisfaction through accomplishment, and to find purpose and meaning in life.

It should come as no surprise, then, that workers at all levels, in all kinds organizations, are bringing their spiritual beliefs and values to work with them, or are seeking to discover new beliefs and values through their work. Many people see work as a place where they can live out their personal spirituality; some see their place of work as their primary spiritual community. We agree. We are trying to build the house of work on the foundation of the rock of wisdom. This brings us to a vital question.

While Buddhism has for thousands of years provided a spiritual foundation for the daily lives of millions around the world, the question is: Does Buddhism have anything to offer us—Buddhists and non-Buddhists alike—in today's world of work? We think it does, and we offer it in this book. Spiritual wisdom, whether it be Western or Eastern, can inspire and instruct us in how to live a good life, a fulfilled, happy life. We offer you the teachings of the Buddha as well as our own application of these teachings to your work situations.

Who was the Buddha?

Buddha was a psychologist and a teacher; he was not a god. He thought of himself more as a doctor, dispensing the medicine of insight—insight into our human problems, both as individuals and as groups. But more than offering insight into our problems, he taught us how to transcend them. Beginning with his own experience of enlightenment or awakening, he created a system of thought—the Buddhist tradition—that provides helpful, practical answers to typical human situations we face in our work lives today. Buddhism is, above all, useful. It is not about pie in the sky; it is about here and now. It is not about theory; it is about *practice*. It is not just a way of thinking; it is a way of being and *doing*.

What would Buddha do? is the question we ask in this book—applying it to problems with bosses, coworkers, customers, and others. We also apply it to dealing with ourselves—since many of us are our own worst enemies when it comes to finding peace and satisfaction at work.

Buddha strove to alleviate suffering and find happiness. Who doesn't? Buddha struggled with life just as we do today, and he discovered the keys to living. He sought to teach his discoveries to others, and we seek to continue his teachings by sharing them with you.

The Buddha in you

This book is founded on the belief that Buddha was not just a historical figure who lived some 2500 years ago. We believe that, in a profound sense, Buddha also exists within each of us at every moment. Buddha exists in the Buddha Mind, awakening itself, the dawning of insight in each of us. To ask ourselves, *What would Buddha do?* is to ask that source of insight for sacred guidance, to tap into the Buddha consciousness that lies sleeping within us, waiting to be awakened. We've all had moments of awakening, when something has roused the Buddha consciousness from slumber; moments when we've lived outside our limited selves, in union with all things, flowing with the unending current of life. In such moments we experience our true nature, fundamentally interrelated with all living things, and ultimately free from the cages of our ego selves, cages we've strengthened for protection every year of our lives. When we think and act with this freedom we don't just act like Buddhas, we *become* Buddhas.

In writing this book, we have drawn from a wide variety of Buddhist texts, both ancient and contemporary. The dharma (Buddhist truth, Buddhist teaching) has grown through the centuries, as Buddhist writers and thinkers have shared their Buddha consciousness with us. In this way Buddhism is a living philosophy taught by those who seek awakening in their own lives. A contemporary haiku is just as relevant and legitimate as a sacred scroll by an ancient monk. Each writer expands the dharma in his or her own work. We humbly try to expand the dharma in ours here.

This book aims to help you be the Buddha that you already are, to find your own Buddha Nature and to allow that Nature to guide you in your workday activities. The Buddha in you is your best teacher. It is our hope that the questions and answers we've outlined here will help you bring that Buddha to life.

Using this book

Our book is divided into three main sections: The first section, "Becoming an Enlightened Worker," covers Buddha's wisdom for *individuals*, including such things as how to choose right livelihood, how to be a good employee, and how to be successful. The second section, "Cultivating Enlightened Work Relationships," focuses on how to work with *other people*, including bosses, coworkers, work teams, difficult people, and customers. The third section, "Creating an Enlightened Workplace," deals with broad *organizational* topics, including policies and procedures, human resource issues, technology, work processes, and organizational problems.

If you are totally new to Buddha, you might want to go to the end of the book and read the Appendices first—they'll give you an overview of Buddha's life and teachings. They'll also suggest further resources for strengthening your grasp of Buddhism. But you don't *have* to read these at all; we've written this book so that Buddha's basic teachings are embedded right in the chapters.

If you have a specific work problem on which you'd like some guidance, you can look up your problem in the Table of Contents and go straight to that answer. Of course, we can't list every possible situation in one little book, but we think we've covered many of the problems you face in your work.

We have written for the broadest possible audience, from frontline workers to supervisors and managers to senior executives. There is wisdom and guidance here for entrepreneurs and small businesses, as well as Fortune 500 companies. Many of the ideas here apply to non-profit organizations as well as for-profit businesses. But of course, not all answers will be equally useful to all readers. Some are directed more to managers and business owners, while others are directed more to employees. But remember, we are all in this game of work together, so you may gain by reading answers that at first glance seem not to apply to you. If you're a manager, you're an employee, too. Reading advice to employees will remind you of that and remind you what you're asking of your employees. Employees, for their part, sometimes aspire to become managers; you can begin to learn what this means by reading management answers and seeing how hard it is to be a good boss.

Buddha isn't here to answer our specific questions, but we have done our best to understand his teachings and apply them as he would if he were here. Some of these teachings are general and philosophical, while others are more detailed and specific. That's because some workplace problems are basic or universal, so we can point to basic and universal solutions, while other problems are more complex or involved and require more pragmatic, how-to answers. The wide variety of questions and answers in this book reflects the wide variety of situations we face in the different jobs, different organizations, different times, and different places of our careers. Our lives require a richness of answers—some that may even sound contrary to others—and the Buddhist tradition has, over 2500 years, generated this richness in response to a diversity of cultural needs and values.

Finally, it is important that you not accept Buddha's teachings just because he was the Buddha. He was the first one to tell his followers to think for themselves, to question his teachings and test them against their own experience and understanding. We tell you the same. Test the Buddha's teachings and test this book's. Your path is unique to you and ultimately only *you* can decide what advice is useful and what advice isn't. In offering you this book, we invite you to think of it as a buffet. Please take what you want.

A note about inclusive language

It is true that Buddha failed to be fully egalitarian in his teaching and his use of language. Though he did a great deed by allowing women to be nuns, he seems to have done it against his own desires. Though he clearly thought women could be awakened, he continually taught using male examples. Should we fault Buddha for this? One of the ten great Mahayana precepts is not to fault others. Instead, let us say we believe Buddha did a lot more good for women than any of his contemporaries—maybe more than any of ours. We will continue his work by changing his exclusive language to inclusive language.

Long ago, Franz thought he could use "he" and also mean "she." He discovered words are too strong: writing "he" means "he." BJ likes using "they" because, after all, we are all one and the same, not separate individuals, according to Buddhist philosophy. But "they" is not quite right for "he" or "she" either. And we all know that none of us is an "it," so, where does that leave us? We will simply alternate "she" and "he" in this book. We trust Buddha would approve.

Part 1

Becoming An Enlightened Worker

To study the Buddha Way is to study the self.

Dogen Zenji, Genjo Koan

A great beauty of Buddha's teachings is how they always return our attention to us, to our minds. Mind creates the world. This means you can follow the path of awakening, no matter what anyone else around you is doing. Your awakening and growth are not contingent upon others. You might find this thought frightening, you might find it liberating.

Some people want to put their faith and future in others' hands:

- "Just tell me what to do, boss, and I'll do it," they say.
- "Leaders are supposed to have the answers; that's what they get paid the big bucks for," they emphasize.
- "I just work here; I don't make the rules," they deflect.

For such people, realizing that fate, or karma, lies solely in their own hands can be very upsetting. Many of us are like this.

Others may find Buddha's message terrifically empowering:

- "You get out of it what you are willing to put into it," they suggest.
- "If I own the problem, I also own the solution," they point out.
- "I create my own future, through my thinking, my decisions, my actions, and my attitude," they assert.

For these people, the profoundly personal nature of awakening is exciting and following its path is deeply satisfying. These are the lucky, the *bodhisattvas* (beings who are focused on awakening).

But most of us feel mixed emotions about the prospect and path of becoming enlightened workers. Sometimes we feel great, eager to embark, devoted to continuing. At those times we, too, are bodhisattvas. Other times, we feel discouraged, in need of guidance, spiritually inadequate. That is when we need help.

In this section, we apply Buddha's words to every phase of work. You may be discouraged trying to find the right job. You may be shaky in marshalling the many strengths your work demands. You might be looking for new solutions to old problems. Or you might simply be looking for confirmation of the work values you already hold. Maybe your own Buddha nature is already well-awakened. Whatever your interest or need, Buddha has wisdom for you. His example and his teaching can help you bring your spiritual life to work, and bring your work to life.

In these answers, Buddha often returns to two fundamental teachings. First, no one is inadequate. Each of us has the Buddha nature within. Second, we always have a choice. To be awake is always optional. Mindful, or mindless—our decision.

Choosing Enlightened Work

Creating Right Livelihood

What would Buddha say about the advantages of enlightened work?

> *Since there is nothing to attain, the Bodhisattva lives by the perfection of wisdom with no hindrance in the mind; no hindrance and therefore no fear.*

The Heart Sutra

What are the advantages of enlightened work? Buddha would simply say they're the advantages of enlightenment, because enlightened work brings enlightenment to the workplace. So the question becomes: "Enlightenment, what's that?"

The first person to see Buddha after he was enlightened asked, "Who are you?" Buddha said, "I am awake." Enlightenment is being awake to the moment and the world.

That awakening, that enlightenment, is the goal of Buddhism and there is no reason it cannot be the goal of work as well. Enlightened work, then, wakes up the workplace and the world. The Heart Sutra describes spiritual practices, but it could just as easily describe work practices. It's not about attaining anything; it's about being there, at work or at home, without hindrance and without fear.

"Which comes first," you might ask, "Enlightenment or enlightened work?" Well, where are you, right now? Do the work of the moment. Take a first step. Sure, a first step is not a whole journey; nor is a first answer a whole book.

What would Buddha do about developing a vision and mission for himself?

Living beings are numberless, I vow to save them;
Desires are inexhaustible, I vow to abandon them;
Dharma gates are countless, I vow to enter them;
The Buddha way is unsurpassable, I vow to embody it.

The Four Great Mahayana Vows

Almost all organizations have a mission statement, and some have a vision statement as well. Leaders know the importance of having such things in writing as a compass to guide our values and priorities, to prevent our becoming lost in the details of day-to-day organizational issues. Organizations that are built to last operate on a handful of key values, principles, or beliefs, that guide everything they do: policies, goals, hiring, training, marketing, spending, and every other aspect of work life.

Successful individuals also have *personal* mission statements, or creeds, by which they live their lives. Millions of practicing Buddhists make the Four Great Vows every day, to remind themselves of the commitments they have made: commitment to respect all forms of life; commitment to break free of the tyranny of endless desires; commitment to continuous study and learning; commitment to bring their Buddha nature into their lives in every way. Of course the more beautiful the goal, the smaller the chance we shall accomplish it. No matter, the commitment is to *try*. Don't sell yourself short. What is your vision or mission for your *own* life? You can make that vision inseparable from your work. It can be the heart of your personal mission statement.

How would Buddha choose the right career or job?

> *A birdcatcher asked the Teacher, "My family's always been birdcatchers. If we stop, we'll starve. But doing this (evil) work, can I still reach Buddhahood?"*
>
> *The Teacher answered, "The mind goes to hell, not the body. So when you kill a bird, take your mind and kill it too. Doing this, you can reach Buddhahood."*
>
> **Zen Teacher Bankei**

Almost everyone at one time or another has asked the general question: "How do I find the right career, the right job, where I will be fulfilled and happy?" If you are seeking to learn from Buddha's teachings, this question is especially important because part of the very core of Buddhism, the Eightfold Noble Path, is Right Livelihood. Simply put, that means doing work that helps, rather than harms, all living things. As Buddha brought work into the spiritual life, he brought spirituality into worklife. Right Livelihood is being Buddha at work.

For many people, this is a serious problem. What if you work for a company that makes instruments of destruction? What if you work for an organization whose fundamental mission is not aligned with your own values? Can you still do enlightened work? Can you still pursue Right Livelihood?

Buddha's answer here is very interesting. He taught that we should try hard never to harm other living things, and yet here Zen Teacher Bankei reconciles enlightenment with birdcatching. How can this be? The key issue, it seems, is not so much what your body is doing, but what your mind is doing. Of course, the mind and the body are intimately connected, and one usually follows the other in day-to-day life. But this need not always be so. It is possible to have the body engaged in one activity, and the mind focused on something else. Here, he advises the bird catcher to kill the bird if he absolutely must (he recognizes that people have to make a living), while keeping the mind not on killing the bird (which would be wrong livelihood) but on killing the mind, that is, killing desire and attachment. A creative solution, and one that acknowledges the power of our environment over us. There are times we cause harm without meaning to.

Of course, Buddha would never accept this as a long-term solution. He would encourage the birdcatcher to change jobs if he could. Birdcatching simply is not Right Livelihood. But perhaps for the time being there is no choice. You must feed yourself and your family, and this means you must make a living in a compromised fashion. You'll simply have to work that much harder to keep your mind pure until you can find work that *is* Right Livelihood.

You can pursue enlightenment no matter what job you have, and you can often transform your boring or unfulfilling work into enlightened work by changing how you *think* about your work, by changing your spirit. You can be a garbage collector, in the spirit of love and service, and be well on your way to Buddhahood. There's no question that garbage collecting is Right Livelihood, while a creative and high-paying position in a corrupt and greedy field is not. Whatever your job is, start there; adopt the right mind and take that first step on the path. Yes, the path may lead you to change careers, but Buddha does not demand you harm yourself in doing so. In the end, only a career that helps will make you truly fulfilled.

What would Buddha say about attachment and desire at work?

Don't cling to what is pleasant or unpleasant.
Suffering missing the first, getting the second.
Liking things just hurts too much; don't do it.
For he is free who has no likes or hates.

Dhammapada 210–211

Perhaps the central tenet of Buddhism is that attachment is the root of all suffering. When we hold something dear, when we love it a lot, we will suffer if we become separated from it. It is unwise to love a job too much, to love an organization too much, or to be too attached to having a particular job or career. For if you cannot attain it, or if you attain it and then lose it, you suffer greatly.

The same is true for being attached to *not* having certain things at work. If something is unpleasant to me, I will do everything I can to avoid it, or if it comes my way anyway, to get rid of it. What is unpleasant might be a person I don't want to work with, a task I don't like to do, a responsibility I don't want to assume, a boss whom I detest, or anything else I resist or avoid. I will suffer greatly, to the extent that I am attached to *not* having certain things or people in my worklife.

Buddha's path offers me freedom from suffering at work, and everywhere else, too. All I need do is to wake up, to notice that things come and go in my life, and to practice being unattached to any of them. Good things come into my work life, and good things leave. Bad things come into my work life, and bad things leave. That's the secret: everything in my work life is transitory; it will change; it will pass away. Find your freedom in that, and remember that nothing says you cannot be an agent of that change yourself. Finding this freedom is not easy; society constantly pulls us away from it. But Buddha found it, and so can you.

What would Buddha do to become a great employee?

> *A good employee serves her employer in five ways: by getting up and starting work before her; by stopping after her; by taking from her employer only what is given; by striving to do her work well; and by upholding her employer's name.*

Digha Nikaya 31

If you're wondering what you can do to endear yourself to the boss, to be a fabulous employee, Buddha has some words of wisdom for you. Get back to basics. Forget about kissing up—no one is impressed by that. To be a great employee, start by doing great work. Here are five suggestions from Buddha:

1. Get up and start work before your boss. It never hurts to arrive at work a little bit early; you will be calm and collected as you start your day; and things will be perking along by the time your boss arrives.

2. Stop working after your boss: being willing to stay a little longer to tie up loose ends, or to help a coworker, is a great way to show your boss that you are willing to "go the extra mile." And so often, this quieter time is the most productive in the day.

3. Take from your employer only what is given. It may seem harmless to take home that pencil or that wrench or some other little thing, but it really *is* stealing and it's the first step

on a long road down. Everyone may do it, but you don't want to be just like everyone, do you? Isn't that the point here?

4. Strive to do your work well. This may seem like a no-brainer, but you'd be surprised how many people do just enough work to get by and then wonder why they aren't doing better in their careers. Don't waste your effort on scheming or daydreaming; Buddha always focused on effort. Here's the bottom line: above all else, do great work!

5. Uphold your employer's name. To many people you meet, you *are* your company; whether you are on the job or off, speak well of your employer and represent them well in the community; it will come back to reward you in surprising ways. If you care about your company, honor its name.

What does it take to be a great employee? You can always add more things to this list, of course, but Buddha lays it out plain: start with the basics. There's no place to go but up.

What would Buddha do to bolster employee self-esteem?

As a solid rock doesn't quaver in the wind,
So the wise are moved by neither praise nor blame.

Dhammapada 81

You may have heard that Buddha denied the existence of the self. Let's be clear: Buddha never denied that we experience the world and our lives through a sense of self. This self matters and needs attention. What Buddha denied was the *enduring* nature of this self: it is not eternal. Our selves arise and they pass away; and in fact, even while they exist, they only do so in relationship with others.

Buddha respects the need for self-esteem. The self in this world needs to feel positive about itself. He warns you not to be swayed by other people's opinion of you or your work. You know when you have done your best work, and you are the best person to judge your own actions. Do not give away your self-confidence by letting others' opinions determine whether you feel good or bad about yourself. If you let others' praise, or criticism affect your sense of self-worth, you will forever be a slave to public opinion. In a sense, what they think of you is none of your business. Does a rock care what the wind thinks of it? A rock just goes on doing its thing.

It is a truism that people who feel good about themselves produce good results. It is also true that people who produce good results feel good about themselves. So, which comes first, the self-esteem or the good results?

Buddha would tell us it doesn't matter which comes first. If you feel good about yourself, chances are you are already producing good results. If you don't feel good about yourself, try producing good results and see how your self-esteem improves. Instead of the contemporary "power of positive thinking," Buddhism emphasizes the "power of positive doing." Get into action, and see how it improves your mood, sometimes immediately. Action alleviates anxiety. It also helps elevate self-esteem, and can even lighten a depression. So, if your self-esteem isn't all you'd like it to be, get your butt in gear. We're not sure Buddha would say it that way, but that's what he'd be thinking.

What would Buddha advise about self-improvement?

*As the smith burns out the silver's dross,
So the wise man burns away his own.*

Dhammapada 239

Walking the path of awakening is about progress, not perfection. Buddha might well have been the spiritual father of Edward Deming, preaching the gospel of continuous improvement and incremental progress. Deming focused his attention on refining work processes, while Buddha focused his attention on refining human beings. But they would agree that improvement never ends.

You notice, in the quote above, that Buddha teaches each individual to be responsible for his own improvement. It is not your boss's job to make you into a better worker and a better person. It is your job. Your boss and other teachers may help you by giving you instruction, coaching, and feedback, but ultimately *you* are responsible for your own continuous improvement.

A fool ignores his responsibility, throwing up his hands and exclaiming, "I am what I am." He has accepted his character as his fate. But the wise person says, "I can change; I can improve; I can grow toward anything I want to be, if I am willing to work. I can follow the path and awaken." Buddhists say this human life is rare and precious; use it well.

What would Buddha do to stay focused?

Like a fish on land, flopping, gasping,
The mind contorts to flee the tempter's power.
To train this jerky, willful mind is better;
The trained and ordered mind at last can rest.

Dhammapada 34–35

Buddha wasn't a licensed psychiatrist or psychologist, but he understood human nature. We might chuckle at his imagery in describing the human mind like a fish on dry land, slippery, hard to get ahold of, flipping this way and that with no apparent pattern or direction. We also might find this a little scary, for the future of this fish is not good. Some people call this "monkey mind," always jumping around, chattering. Some people call it attention deficit disorder. Whatever you call it, we all have it, to a greater or lesser degree.

So, if we all have short attention spans and are easily distracted, what can we do to focus in order to see projects through to completion? Buddha advises us to train our minds, specifically through meditation and other forms of spiritual discipline. A trained mind is good because it lets us to focus on the important things. A trained mind brings ease because it is uncluttered. We no longer feel the anxiety of the monkey mind, chattering endlessly, or the fish mind, gulping for the lost sea.

So, take up a spiritual practice to train your mind. Whether this is a martial art like Aikido, a meditation practice like TM, a yoga discipline like hatha yoga, a devotional practice like reciting scripture and prayers, or some other variety, is not important—just practice *something*. The practice trains the mind, and a trained mind is a good thing. Your best choice is to look around and pick something you *like*. Training in a way you *like*, you'll simply *do* more.

Within the confines of this book, we can't train your mind for you, but here's one suggestion for beginners: When you feel distracted or angry or sleepy, acknowledge it; don't deny it. That begins the training: react to the negative with the positive. Now, strengthen the positive by bringing the mind back to breathing. Stop moving; relax. Take a deep breath. Don't think, just feel the breath. Don't try to breathe any special way, just breath naturally and let your mind rest in that breathing. You can count your breaths if it helps you. Count to ten. Let the myriad things rest. Now come back to the moment. You have trained yourself to find strength in the face of distraction. Now take the strength of that focus on the breath and apply it to your task.

Practical Enlightenment

Chop Wood, Carry Water

How would Buddha establish priorities?

*The wise person, who hurries when it's time to hurry,
and who slows his pace down when slowness is the
thing, is deeply happy because he's got priorities in line.*

Theragatha 161

Peter Drucker, the grandfather of today's management consultants and business thinkers, says the challenge of the modern manager is that he knows there are ten things needing to be done, but he has time to do only six. He's got to pick the right six to do, then go home at night and not worry about the four he had to let go.

Buddha would tell us Drucker's statement applies to everyone, not just managers. We work in fast-motion, and there are many demands on our time. The task is not somehow to find more time, but rather to make the most of the time we have. Our real challenge is not short time, but effective prioritization.

We must each choose what is most important to our happiness and to our success, in life and in work. Once we have made our choices, our daily actions follow from those choices. Instead of racing around frantically, treating everything like an emergency, we hurry when it is appropriate—but we slow down when that is appropriate. This is harder than it sounds. We make different choices and have different insights in these different speed modes. We need to use both in enlightened work.

What would Buddha do about time management?

> *Yunmen addressed his monks and said, "I do not ask about before the 15th of the month; tell me about after the 15th." Nobody said anything, so he answered himself: "Every day is a good day."*

The Blue Cliff Record 6

Zen Teacher Yunmen does not ask his people about the past; he knows the past is gone and there is nothing anyone can do about it. Yet he is not asking about the future, either, for he also knows that no one can predict the future. He is testing to see if they are worrying uselessly about time, past or future. Concerned and perplexed, the monks do not answer.

Perhaps we can do better. Yunmen is trying to teach them (and us) it is pointless to expend energy lamenting the past or worrying about the future, when we cannot control either one. It is pointless to divide up our years and days, living as if we were calendars. From a pure Zen perspective, there *is* no future or past. We're not like calendars—we're more like clocks. We tell the time as it happens. Our hands are always pointing to NOW. There is no 15th, nor any day before or after. All we really have to work with is today, and today is a good day.

When Buddha tells us to "have a nice day," he is not making small talk, he means it. This is the heart of effective time management.

What would Buddha do about procrastination?

"It's too cold, too hot, too late."
With excuses like these,
People shirk their work,
And the moment passes them by.

Theragatha 3.5

Who among us isn't guilty of procrastination? It's so seductive and seems so harmless when we succumb to it. "Oh, I'll get to that project later. I don't have time to do it now." "Who can work in this heat?" "I'll make those phone calls tomorrow. It's too late in the day; I'm sure everyone's already gone home." "I'll just take care of these little things first, and save the big one for when I have a bigger chunk of time." Sure, uh-huh. Some of these reasons may even hold a grain of truth. Unfortunately, all too many times, the window of opportunity closes, and we kick ourselves (or someone else does) for having missed our chance.

The wise person knows the dangers of procrastination and resists the siren song that tells her to put off 'til tomorrow. Put off things, even once, and you begin to establish a pattern. If others, feeling lazy, accept it, you begin to create a whole culture of procrastination. Your team begins to lag behind. In place of this, the wise person does things NOW, making the moment count. Acting mindfully in the moment, we stay ahead of the curve and are able to set the terms; we flow with the Tao. If Buddha spoke Latin he would surely have said "Carpe diem!"

What would Buddha say about contributing ideas at work?

If he doesn't speak up, others can't know him;
he's a wise man lost among fools.

Anguttara Nikaya 2.51

Buddha is saying a mind is a terrible thing to waste. If you have good ideas, you had better share them at work, not keep them to yourself. It is in your best interest, as well as the best interest of your organization, to contribute in every way you can, whenever you can. If you don't, you're just a fool among fools. No one knows your wisdom.

Or, as former Vice President Dan Quayle sagely offered, "What a waste it is to lose one's mind. Or not to have a mind is being very wasteful. How true that is." The Buddha Mind is in us all (even Mr. Quayle). We think he was demonstrating it here, for surely he meant that losing one's wisdom among a crowd of fools is a terrible waste. Retain your presence of mind. We all must speak up, even ex–vice presidents.

What's that? You complain that they don't pay you for your great ideas? There is no reward for contributing good suggestions? Nonsense, Buddha says. You are thinking too narrowly. You've heard that virtue is its own reward—well, awakening is, too. Bonuses are nice, promotions are nice, but awakening is nicer.

What would Buddha tell us about keeping commitments?

As bright but scentless flowers that bear no fruit,
Are words of one who leaves them unfulfilled.
But as scented flowers bearing fruit,
Are words of one who carries them to fruition.

Dhammapada 51–52

Like so many spiritual teachers, Buddha created metaphors that resound. Here a flower gives color, but no scent. Something important is missing, just as something important is missing in a promise that has no follow-through. This is a simple answer, and fundamental to business as well as spiritual life.

Have you ever had the experience of seeing a gorgeous bloom on a plant and eagerly sniffing the bloom to savor its scent, only to be let down when it has no fragrance? The blossom is still beautiful to the eye, yet the full experience is diminished.

But such disappointment is only a fraction of the letdown we feel when someone makes a commitment to us and then does not follow through. Words are hollow, talk is cheap, and promises are not taken seriously when we see no action behind fine words. No matter how beautiful, words are fruitless and barren if they aren't commitments.

Buddha lived in the real world. He says keep your promises, honor your commitments, and reap the fruit of good relationships with others, at work and at home.

What would Buddha think about the claim that "the ends justify the means"?

Through tainted means, even if for others,
The righteous does not want success that way.

Dhammapada 84

Buddha knows that "the ends justify the means" is a rationalization. And rationalization is just a fancy word for the lies born of the incredible creativity of our monkey minds as they scheme to get things we desire, while keeping our self-esteem intact. To keep up the rationalization, we delude ourselves with phony justifications. Buddha censures this. The *results* we achieve at work are important, but so, too, is the *way* in which we achieve them. No matter how noble our purpose, how lofty our goal, if we lie, cheat, or steal to accomplish that goal, we have essentially sold our souls for success.

How do you know if you are using unrighteous means to accomplish something? That's what being awake is all about. Being conscious of what you are doing in each moment helps ensure that your internal moral compass will warn you when you are violating your own integrity. Are you comfortable describing your actions to your coworkers? to your friends? to your spouse? to your child? Your Buddha nature is always comfortable. If you're not, it's because you've turned away from your Buddha nature. Instead, turn away from actions that force you to rationalize.

Ends and means are both important. But if you can't achieve good ends by good means, let the ends go. No money, status, or goal is worth the price of your own good karma, not even goals for the sake of others. Good people don't want tainted offerings.

How would Buddha take care of company property?

Parking this car, carefully, attentively,
I vow to help all beings to their resting place.

Tassajara Zen Mountain Center Gatha

Buddhism is a way of life. It is being mindful, as fully aware as you can be, every moment, doing ordinary things. Driving a company car, using the office phone, eating in the company cafeteria, sitting at company desks in company chairs, using pencils, computers, clocks, machines and equipment owned by the organization—*nothing* is too trivial or inconsequential to be on the Buddha Way.

So, how should I treat company property? Well, just what is the difference between company property and my own? They are so interrelated there is no final difference. Nor are either different from the whole world. Every car can follow the Middle Way. Every pencil can write a sutra. Every chair, and every butt in it, is Buddha. I vow to help it rest.

Becoming Successful
&
Making Money

Mantra or Mammon?

What would Buddha advise about "playing it close to the vest"?

> Herons, cats, and burglars,
> By moving silently and carefully,
> Accomplish what they set out to do.
> Bodhisattvas also work this way.

Bodhicharyavatara 5.73

Bodhisattvas are people who choose the path of ongoing awakening in all aspects of their lives. They work at it simply and quietly. They focus intently on their goals and objectives, keeping their eyes on the prize. They do not make a big public fuss about what they are up to, bragging or making grandiose proclamations of intent. Instead, they focus their attention like a laser and proceed strategically and deliberately. They are careful in their work, watching every step so that they do not misstep and miss the goal. They do not let themselves get distracted by the commotion around them, by the deeds and misdeeds of others.

Look at the metaphors here. Buddha's metaphor comes from hunting for food or pursuing gain at great risk. Our metaphor comes from poker, where you need to keep your cards and your emotions under wraps. Hunters and gamblers know the stakes and earn respect through their quiet attention. Let us be bodhisattvas and employ that same attention to higher goals.

How would Buddha help people achieve their goals?

He constantly abandons useless mindsets and cultivates useful mindsets. He is resolute and concentrated in his effort. He never abandons his efforts toward achieving useful mindsets.

Anguttara Nikaya 5.53

Buddha understood that most human beings are easily distracted, and inclined to take multitasking to ridiculous extremes. Buddha's way is quiet, simple; he teaches it because he knows the power of concentration, self-discipline, and focus. He is really the spiritual father to some of today's "success writers," whose bestsellers teach us how to manifest our dreams and achieve our goals. These authors are tapping into what Buddha knew 2500 years ago: that the mind has immense power, if only its owner would use it well.

Buddha urges us to keep laser-like focus (okay, they didn't have lasers in Buddha's day; he called it "onepointed mind") on our vision or objective—to be unwavering in our concentration. A man with a mission does not dissipate and waste energy on useless distractions.

Buddha teaches us that quiet intensity—focusing all energy and attention on the desired goal—begins inside and is all that is required for success. Set your mind toward your goals. Evaluate what are useful mindsets for you. Stick to them. Yes, this is hard; useless mindsets are often enjoyable. But they are also a waste of time. Never abandon your effort!

What would Buddha do about finding the "right" answer to a problem?

If you claim a position, you don't have the correct view.

Instructions from Manjushri

The answer to our question is a paradoxical one: There *is* no one right answer (correct view) to a problem or situation. As soon as we think we have the right answer, we are mistaken. But more deeply, it's not the answer that is mistaken—the mistake happens inside *us*, when we think we can definitively find a permanent answer. Since everything in life is always changing, the correct view today might be incorrect tomorrow. The right answer to a problem changes from day to day, because the problem itself is always changing.

Jean Kerr, the playwright, has said, "If you can keep your head about you when all about you are losing theirs, it's just possible you haven't grasped the situation." These are wise words. Feeling anxious or unsettled is understandable when things are changing as fast as they are today. No one can stay on top of things all the time.

Frustrating, isn't it? We humans want so very much to comfort ourselves with absolutes, to be reassured that we have the right answer. But if Buddha is correct, and all is changing, we have to live with the anxiety and uncertainty this brings. It's a choice: we can put ourselves to sleep by clinging to absolutes ("this is the only right way"), or we can wake up and see that we must be limber and flexible, always in flux, always changing, and always needing to find changing answers to changing problems.

What would Buddha do about admitting mistakes?

All the evil karma created by me from of old,
on account of my beginningless greed, hatred and
ignorance,
born of my deeds, words and thoughts,
I now confess openly and fully.

Zen Gatha of Purification

Confession is good for the soul. Or, confession is good for the karma. Confession requires both honesty and humility, both of which we need.

Admitting you were wrong, or you made a mistake, is the first important step to improvement—both self-improvement and improvement on any work project. People who never admit mistakes never get to learn from them. They are doomed to keep repeating them until someone *else* finds them out. People who admit mistakes are already on their way to making fewer of them in the future. Good bosses know this. They know *everyone* makes mistakes and so they trust people who admit them. That's how to build working relationships.

Look at what is happening in this verse: purification. Not only does admitting mistakes begin the process of learning from them, it also begins the process of correcting them, of purifying ourselves of them. When we repeat the verse of purification we admit our tainted past, but in admitting that taint, we also acknowledge we see it from a better perspective. Seeing our greed, hatred, and ignorance, we also see our generosity, love, and wisdom. Admitting our mistakes is also admitting our potential for greatness.

What would Buddha do to get promoted?

High rank depends on circumstances; is only gained through effort; yet is effortlessly lost. It does not lead to contentment or happiness, still less to peace of mind.

Jatakamala 8.53

Buddha did not work for promotions and neither should you. Getting that promotion is not going to make your life great and it's not going to be permanent, given today's rapid pace of change. A promotion comes with circumstances and circumstances can take it away. No, the ultimate destination of the Buddhist path is not the top of the organizational ladder. Buddha wouldn't do anything special to get promoted.

But here's the paradox: there is nothing wrong with getting promoted, either. Buddha got promoted all the time. Buddha was a privileged aristocrat, then a respected young ascetic with followers, and ultimately became the head of a whole religion. He was not afraid of rising to the top and neither should you be. It's just that he never cared about rank or promotion. Instead he cared about—he was utterly committed to—doing his work with brilliance. Buddha understood that getting promoted is a happy side-effect of doing excellent work, and he never confused the two.

Where does that leave you on the career ladder? Here's the thing: reaching the top isn't as important as you think. What is going to give you contentment, happiness, and peace of mind, is what gave those things to Buddha: deep insight into the wonderful interdependence of things, the opportunity to make a contribution to your organization, and the chance to use your skills fully. So do your very best work, and who knows?—perhaps you'll even get promoted.

What would Buddha teach about dressing for success?

What good is matted hair and cloaks, you fool!
Your insides are tangled, yet you comb your surface!

Dhammapada 394

Buddha does not have anything against dressing well, per se. But don't confuse *looking* good with *being* good.

In Buddha's day, the Brahmins, the priestly elite, were recognizable by their fine cloaks and their distinctive matted hairstyles. But Buddha knew that just looking the part did not make you wise. In the text above, we see Buddha chiding a dullard, who is obsessed with his natty appearance, when he should be paying attention to his mental and spiritual development. If your inside's a mess, no amount of grooming or finery is going to clean you up. But if you're clean within, that will shine through whatever you're wearing. No one ever talks about what Buddha *wore*, but they do talk about his radiant appearance.

Likewise today, it's what's on the *inside* that counts in terms of success at work. What skills and talents do you have to contribute? Do you work well with others? Are you honest and hard-working? Do you have integrity? Are you compassionate and kind? Have you tamed your mind so that you are focused and effective? Do you have self-discipline?

So, before you run right out and buy that Armani suit for your next big job interview, take a good look in the closet of your mind and character. That's where the *real* dress for success happens.

How would Buddha celebrate success?

When my success is talked about at work,
I'm quick to have everyone jump in.
But when it's others getting compliments,
I just don't feel like joining in the fun.

Bodhicharyavatara 6.79

We're so happy to revel in our own successes, we think everyone should just join right in. But how slow we are to join in celebrating the success of others! We pretend to be happy, but we feel resentful inside. With our bosses in particular, we often revert to childish attitudes, wanting to be Daddy's favorite, and resenting the praise and attention Daddy/boss lavishes on coworkers/siblings. Of course, we would never admit this out loud, but we feel it. We are like greedy children, fearful that we won't get our share of the good stuff.

Buddha would point out that, once again, we are succumbing to the illusion that we are separate from one another; our misperception leads us to resent others' success. "If the pinkie successfully removed the wax from your ear, the index finger wouldn't be resentful, would it?" Buddha might ask us with a smile. Businesses ought to be as cooperative as hands. There is plenty of success to go around, and each person has the opportunity to be successful in his or her own way. How much happier we are when we celebrate everyone's successes as our own! And how much nicer we are to be with. Bosses notice *that*, too.

What would Buddha call "the root of all evil"?

> *Manjushri: What is the root of good and evil?*
> *Vimalakirti: Physicality is the root of good and evil.*
> *Manjushri: What is the root of physicality?*
> *Vimalakirti: Desire is the root of physicality.*
> *Manjushri: What is the root of desire?*
> *Vimalakirti: The false self is the root of desire.*
> *Manjushri: What is the root of the false self?*
> *Vimalakirti: Ignorance is the root of the false self.*
> *Manjushri: What is the root of ignorance?*
> *Vimalakirti: Emptiness.*
> *Manjushri: What is the root of emptiness?*
> *Vimalakirti: When something is empty, what root can it have?*
> *So all things grow from an empty root.*

Vimalakirtinirdesha Sutra 7

This dialogue between two awakened beings brings out our real relationship with money. It evokes St. Paul's statement in the Bible, that love of money is the root of all evil. But the Buddhist teaching goes deeper. Our desire for money goes beyond the nature of money, even beyond the nature of desire itself. It points to the nature of all things.

Manjushri, the bodhisattva of wisdom, begins with a question asked all over the world: What is the root of all evil? The great householder bodhisattva, Vimalakirti, answers right away that not greed, not money, but focus on physicality is the root. In this, Buddha teaches something slightly different, but not incompatible with what Jesus taught. Money, even loving it, is not intrinsically evil. Instead, evil comes from our delusion that the physical world is fundamental.

Money responds to and perpetuates this delusion that the physical will satisfy us. In a way, money is the ultimate empty thing: something appearing huge but in fact entirely hollow. It acts to entrap us in pleasures that are themselves empty. We keep score with money, both as individuals and as organizations. We measure success with money, so our earnings and our economies must always grow. Yet this never-ending quest can never be fulfilled.

This entrapment in the physical arises from our desires, our unquenchable yearnings brought on by our ignorant belief in our selves as separate beings. In reality, our selves, and all things, are empty. "Empty" means something special for Buddhists. It means "hollow," having no significance in and of itself, but rather, significant by being connected to everything else. It means not separate, never alone. It means interfused and interdependent with all other beings, all other things.

This has profound implications for our relationship with money. If this is how things really are, money distracts us from what will genuinely give us happiness: the pleasure of experiencing the whole world. The whole world is available right now, for free. You don't need money, you need freedom from desire. Money won't hurt you unless you let it. But unless you are very wise and wonderfully self-aware, be careful that you don't start looking to money for fulfillment it can never bring. The best things in life aren't things.

What would Buddha teach about personal wealth?

> *When a person of integrity becomes wealthy, he provides pleasures and satisfactions for himself, for his parents, for his wife and children, for his underlings, and for his friends. He makes offerings to priests and holy persons, offerings of the highest kind, aiming toward heaven and leading to supreme happiness. When he uses his wealth properly, kings don't take it, thieves don't take it, fire doesn't take it, floods don't take it, and unworthy heirs don't take it. His wealth, used properly, goes to good ends, never to waste.*

Samyutta Nikaya 3.19

Buddha had no problem with people making money, even becoming rich. Personal wealth is not a problem, unless it is not used well. Buddha teaches rich people to be responsible with their wealth by providing for family needs, employee needs, and the needs of friends. He also supports giving to spiritual organizations in order to enrich the spiritual well-being of everyone. In the quote, he emphasizes that good stewardship of money guarantees that one's personal wealth will be secure from threats and loss of all kinds.

This is naturally what a person of integrity does when wealthy. But for many of us, integrity does not always come naturally, especially when we get rich. We are torn between our personal desires and our commitment to live our values. Developing integrity is like developing a muscle—the more you exercise it, the stronger it gets. If our integrity is weak, we can act our way to right thinking. If we act as if we have integrity, in time we really will have it.

What would Buddha tell us about greed?

Even heavenly pleasures don't distract
One who's pleased by ending of desire.

Dhammapada 187

It's a good thing Buddha wasn't around for the "Me Decade" of the 1980s. He wouldn't have liked what he saw: conspicuous consumption, "looking out for #1," and "greed is good" were inescapable attitudes. "Tch, tch, tch," Buddha would have clucked. Buddha would have seen through our mania for possessions to the restless vacancy that lies beneath the sparkling veneer of "have more, be happy."

Mother Teresa once remarked that the spiritual hunger she saw in the Western world was far worse that the physical hunger she saw in India. She, like Buddha, knew that money and things can never make us happy—more things only make us want more things.

Real happiness comes when we become free of our cravings and stop the endless searching for something to fill them. When freed from our greed, we can again delight in pleasures. In fact, we can *truly* delight in pleasures for the first time, since until then pleasure is veiled with the clinging film of desire.

What would Buddha do if he got rich?

That's how it is! Few are those who get rich and yet don't become intoxicated and irresponsible from it, who don't get greedy for sensual delight, who don't mistreat living things.

Samyutta Nikaya 3.6

The person who can get rich and not be ruined by it is rare. Jesus said something like this as well: It is easier to fit a camel (or perhaps a rope) through the eye of a needle than for a rich person to get into heaven. Spiritual teachers work hard to keep us from going astray. They see the seductive poison of money and they want to keep it from us. Buddha himself grew up with endless money and finally had to abandon it completely. He had experienced first-hand how excessive money distorts us.

Money is a great temptation; it deludes us, it cajoles us, it waits us out. It has implacable patience and terrible readiness. If we have irresponsibility or greed in us, it will wait for its chance and entice us to do the wrong thing.

So what would Buddha do if he got rich? He showed us: Buddha turned away from a life of riches. If we don't have the freedom to follow him financially, we must follow him internally. Our minds must be free from the distortion of riches. We cannot be greedy for the power and the sensual indulgence it promotes. We have to treat money like a visitor we respect but also know is dangerous. We greet such a visitor cordially, but do not get too intimate, lest we be seduced. Living this way, we are free to aid the world in ways Buddha never could.

Overcoming Problems

Mind over Matter

What would Buddha do when discouraged and depressed?

> *Once, during a meditation retreat, a student said to the Zen teacher Soen Nakagawa, "I am very discouraged. What should I do?"*
>
> *Soen replied, "Encourage others." This is Zen thinking.*
>
> **Philip Toshio Sudo**, *Zen Computer*, p.67

Philip Toshio Sudo gives us a beautiful vignette from the work of a beloved Zen teacher. It exemplifies Zen thinking by turning away from the eternal troubles of the self and out toward the eternal possibilities of helping others.

Yes, we know this is hard to do. And we know it is hardest to do exactly when you are most burdened by your own discouragement. But that is what is so remarkable about what happens when you do it anyway. You feel better. You may think you have nothing left, nothing to give. But when you have no encouragement for yourself you will be surprised as you discover how you can still find great compassion for others. When your own trouble is right at the surface, you will see their troubles so much more clearly. Lose yourself in helping them. As soon as you do, your own troubles are over.

Will they return? *Of course* they'll return. Troubles come and troubles go; that is the way of things. But it's alright, because in helping others you'll find you'll have helped yourself. It's a miracle.

What would Buddha do about corporate codes of ethics?

If you don't get drunk, no one needs to tell you not to. Rules about what to do and not do only apply to inferior priests and priestesses.

Zen Teacher Bankei

Codes of ethics have become common in organizations. Their existence is a commentary on modern society's growing gap between genuine ethics and mere legality. When technically legal conduct becomes the accepted standard of behavior, it seems codes of ethics are necessary to remind people of true moral standards.

But Zen Teacher Bankei points out the irony of this: such ethics codes only affect inferior priests and middling people. Good priests, and any other good people, don't need to be told all the bad things they shouldn't do. They are not going to do them anyway. Only potential wrongdoers need a specific list of the various wrong things they must refrain from.

If your organization has such a code of ethics for employees, management is insulting the good workers and merely educating the bad ones, not changing them. If you are forced to sign such a code of ethics, Buddha sympathizes with you. Just sign it and move on. If you are an honest, ethical person, it is not meant for you. *Of course* you are going to follow it and go beyond it. The code is for the unethical, dishonest person, and though it is doubtful that signing a piece of paper will make him behave differently, perhaps it will remind him of reasons for doing so.

What would Buddha warn about wanting too much?

Reaching for the silence
he hears
every single sound.

Steve Sanfield,
"A Poem for Those of You
Who Are Sometimes Troubled
by Barking Dogs and Low Flying Jets"

Work, like life, can be such a frustrating paradox! Have you ever noticed that the more you want something, the more it seems to elude you? It's almost as if there is this perverse anti-magnetism that pushes things away from us in exact proportion to the extent that we desire them.

Buddha would laugh. Yes, that's how we live. The more we want something—that promotion, that raise, that new job, that recognition from the boss, that fancy Palm Pilot, etc.—the more we suffer because we are so acutely aware of the lack of what we desire. It may or may not really be eluding us, but in our suffering, it surely *feels* like it is!

What's the answer? Don't reach for the silence; let it come to you. Everything you need you have. Notice that no matter what or how much you have, you always want more. There is always that next new thing. You are insatiable. We are all insatiable. Not only that, when we focus on the desire, we define a situation where nothing else can satisfy us, no matter what it is. Instead we must open ourselves to what *does* come. Want less, accept more.

What would Buddha do when asked to take on a really distasteful job?

Buddha said if we really need to,
We have to do some really nasty things.
But never just because someone has asked.

The Precious Jewel of the Teaching 12, quoting the Ratnavali

Sometimes we are asked to do things at work that we really don't want to do. Somebody has to do the grunt work, and sometimes that some-body is you. The distasteful task might be a special project, or it might be part of your regular duties. Distasteful jobs can include firing people, cutting budgets, dealing with conflicts, cleaning up messes, working with difficult circumstances and/or difficult people. These jobs can be physi-cally nasty, emotionally nasty, morally nasty; every organization has its share of nasty jobs and unpleasant duties that someone has to do.

But nasty jobs raise an interesting question for people following the wisdom of Buddha. He says that just because you are asked to do such a job does not mean you necessarily have to do it. What, is he crazy? How can you *not* do a nasty job you are asked to do at work? What will your boss say?

We all need to shoulder responsibility and we all have to do our share of nasty jobs, but we do not have to do them *all*, and we do not have to do them just because someone asks us. Buddha tells you to ask, "Is this something I really need to do?" Your answer to that question will grow from your answers to its dimensions: Does this job genuinely need to be done? Am I the best person in the organization to do this job? Is doing this job a test I need to pass? And finally, perhaps the most important question: Can I learn from the process of doing this job?

If you can learn from a nasty job, you do need to do it. If the nasty job seems totally pointless and you see no redeeming aspects to it whatsoever, it might be a good idea to have a conversation with your boss and see if you can renegotiate some other arrangement. Easier said than done, granted, but the process of having such a discussion with your boss can be a powerful learning experience in itself. It just may be that the nasty task is not the only learning experience—how you think about and respond to the nasty task may be the *real* learning opportunity.

What would Buddha do about hypocrisy?

I think someone who calls on Amida Buddha when he's gambling and doing other immoral things is trying to take advantage of Amida.

Zen Teacher Bankei

There are few things as disgusting as exhibitions of false piety. This is true no matter what the particular brand of piety—Buddhist, Christian, Jewish, Muslim, Hindu, New Age, 12-Step, whatever. People (or organizations) who make public displays of their religiosity or spirituality while their private behavior is decadent and debauched are just fooling themselves (even if they aren't fooling anyone else!). They certainly aren't fooling whatever deity they worship. Amida is a celestial Buddha who particularly aids those too debauched to help themselves, but only if they're sincere. Amida is not going to send grace to hypocrites. No—hypocrites will reap what they sow, not to worry. That's the power of karma; trust it. Just make sure the hypocrite isn't you.

What would Buddha do about rumors and gossip?

What is Right Speech? Abstaining from lying, divisive speech, abusive speech, and idle chatter.

Samyutta Nikaya 45.8

Buddha did not indulge in rumors or gossip. Right Speech forms part of the Eightfold Path because speech has great power. To follow Buddha's path, we must not engage in talk that divides people, that criticizes people behind their backs, or that is just chatter to kill time. Are rumors and gossip any of these? They're all of these.

Buddha knows you don't mean ill to people when you talk about what's going on with another coworker or another department. You're simply curious, or amused, or disapproving of someone else. But this idle speculation and chatting is almost always destructive. Things get repeated and *always* get distorted in the repeating. By the time a comment has made the full circuit on the company grapevine, it has been totally changed and is completely inaccurate (if it was ever accurate at all).

Trust is impossible in such an environment. Gossip and rumors set an organizational tone in which everyone feels unsafe. People communicate warily because they worry about what others are saying behind their backs. Both gossip and the worry it creates suck up time that could be spent solving problems, cultivating new ideas or exploring new markets. Productivity and profitability are bound to suffer. So, when we indulge in gossip or rumors, we are hurting not only our organization, but also our own future, by undermining the strength of our enterprise.

What would Buddha warn you about the company you keep at work?

If you never meet your equal, travel
Alone. There is no fellowship with fools.

Dhammapada 61

Maybe Mom was a Buddhist . . . she often cautioned, "You're judged by the company you keep." Her words are just as true at work as they are in your personal life. People who work together notice who spends time with whom, and who's in what clique and who's not.

Buddha teaches us to be conscious in every aspect of our day-to-day lives. Just as we should be conscious of what we say and what we do, we need also be conscious of who we are hanging around with at work. If you spend time with gossips and slackers, other people will probably see you as a gossip and slacker too—even if you're not. Chances are, you will be soon.

If you're smart, you'll surround yourself with people you admire and respect. Work is like tennis: if you play with someone better than you, the challenge and stimulation will stretch your game. Work success is the same. Work with others who are smarter and more talented than you; the challenge and stimulation will stretch your work. If you look around and really can't find anyone to learn from, perhaps you're not working in the right place.

Into Your Future

Creating Your Own Karma

What would Buddha tell people who want to change themselves?

One who turns away from recklessness
Is like the moon emerging from the clouds.
Her evil deeds give way to good and she
Is like the moon emerging from the clouds.

Dhammapada 172-173

If Buddha was anything, he was an optimist. "Of course you can change yourself," he would say, "that is what the path of awakening is all about—personal transformation. I am proof, right here in front of you. Here is my life, my teaching, devoted to showing you how to follow me."

Take your first step on this path and you are well on your way. Why? Look at the metaphor Buddha uses here. You are like the moon, *always* shining whether clouds cover your light or not. *Of course* you have it in you to make the changes you desire. If you didn't have the ability, you wouldn't have the desire.

Buddha cheers us on in this passage and he'd cheer anyone on who was ready to do the work of changing herself. It may sound goofy, but Buddha is not just spiritual leader, he's a cheerleader. Try visualizing *that* when you're feeling down.

What would Buddha tell you about making your workday worthwhile?

Strive to make your day productive
Whether in little things or big.
Every day and every night
Bring you closer to your death.

Theragatha 451

You may or may not like your job, but like it or not, your job fills a huge chunk of your day, of your *life*. When a day is gone, it is gone forever. You can't go out and make another for yourself to fill the loss of the one you just wasted. With each passing 24 hours, your life is another day shorter.

Buddha encourages you to make your day productive, no matter if you accomplish big things or little ones. If it were your last day on the job, or on earth, how would you make it meaningful? Would you help a coworker? Would you make sure your work was the best you could do? Would you solve a problem? Would you finally clear off your desk? Would you smile at the janitor and wish him well? Think of all the different ways you can make your day count. They are all available, *today*.

How would Buddha achieve balance between work and personal life?

> *Healthy tension is the natural complementarity of structure and inspiration, responsibility and personal fulfillment, discipline and freedom, authority and egalitarianism, tradition and relevance, male and female, form and void, life and nonexistence. Neglect one side of the pair, and it will turn around and bite.*

Robert Aitken Roshi, *Encouraging Words,* **p.116**

Is life is an either/or proposition, or is it both/and? We live on a continuum of polarities: work versus play, community versus individuality, male versus female, young versus old, task versus relationship, and so on. We live in the dialectical tension between these polar opposites, being pulled in two directions at once. Buddha understood this, and Aitken Roshi reminds us this is not just unavoidable: it is *healthy*.

We must attend to both ends of these polarities. We must spend time alone as well as time in community; we must pay attention to relationships as well as tasks; we must find time for work and for play. Those of us who choose one end of a continuum while ignoring the other never do so successfully, for the neglected end will come back to bite us. If we have too much freedom, we lack the structure and discipline we need to improve ourselves; yet if we have too much structure, we become rigid and stifled with no freedom for inspiration and innovation.

So it is with life inside and outside work. As a scale fulfills its function when its sides are equally balanced, so we humans function best when we balance worklife and personal life—we can be loose, relaxed, capable of movement, just, and fair. This is the Buddha's Middle Way.

What would Buddha do to empower employees?

You must walk; Buddhas just show the path.

Dhammapada 276

Buddha knew that people could think for themselves, could experience life, reflect on it, and test other people's theories or teachings. He explicitly cautioned against blind obedience to authority, against mindless or sentimental allegiance to any guru or teacher, including himself.

This means we all must do the hard work of following our own paths—of taming our minds, focusing our attention, cultivating disciplined work habits, and reflecting on our experiences as we work together. Bosses and teachers or business gurus can help us by pointing the way, but they cannot carry us to the goal. They cannot give us a book or a seminar that transports us to instant nirvana or prosperity. Each and every one of us must travel the road ourselves. If anyone promises you otherwise, he ain't Buddha!

> As Lao Tze, the legendary author of the Tao Te Ching, wrote:
> The Master doesn't talk, he acts. When he's finished his work,
> the people say, "Amazing, we did it all by ourselves!"

Okay, Lao Tze was not a Buddhist. Still, stories have him hanging out with Buddha and we dare anyone to suggest he was not awakened. Besides, both Lao Tze and Buddha knew that talk is cheap. They also knew that people don't listen much to what their bosses *say*, they watch what they *do*. This is how Buddhas and bosses show the way. They embody honesty, integrity, hard work, cooperation, perseverance, skill, and patience. They are role models of how they want employees to behave. Their actions provide examples for others to follow. They don't preach; their work is their message. They lead by becoming workers among workers. This is just how Buddha lived among his followers.

This type of leadership uplifts and empowers followers, who become enrolled in doing great work themselves and immerse themselves in their tasks. The group's work is a seamless operation, with each person doing their best and contributing to the success of the entire group. The work is so transparent that no one can tell where one team member's work ends and another one's starts. Through its work, the group "owns" the final outcome and feels almost as if they have done it with no leader at all. This is true employee empowerment.

What would Buddha say about the cost of integrity and wisdom?

Life is easy for the shameless, cunning,
Corrupt, brazen, nasty, and betraying.
But for one who's honest and insightful,
Trying to pursue purity, it's hard.

Dhammapada 244-245

Why do so few people follow the path of enlightened work? Because it's hard. Buddha levels with us. Living a life of integrity is hard work. Following the path of spiritual growth is hard work. Awakening and staying mindful in each moment requires constant honesty. It's exhausting.

It's much easier to just give in to your worst impulses and let the least common denominator of the workplace drive you. Following a spiritual path at work is like trying to maintain a meticulously clean house while still living in it . . . while a pack of teenagers live in it with you! It takes time, attention, and energy. It's much easier in the short run to live in a laidback, messy house. The teenagers will agree.

But you have to look at the costs and benefits in the long run as well. It's there you'll find that though the cost of integrity is hard work, the cost of giving in is your integrity itself. It's your choice. There is a cost and a payoff to living a life of enlightenment, and there is a cost and a payoff to living the life of a fool. Buddha would tell you to do the math, then decide.

What would Buddha tell us about what's really important in life?

Health is the best gift. Peace the best wealth.
Trust is the best bond. Nirvana happiness.

Dhammapada 204

Buddha was born with the proverbial silver spoon in his mouth. He grew up immersed in wealth and power. He learned first-hand it didn't make him happy—it doesn't make *anyone* happy. Happiness isn't a function of the things you have. Happiness is a function of the person you are. Happiness is an inside job.

All the great spiritual teachers echo Buddha's teachings: what's really important in life are all the things money can't buy you—not just love, but health, peace of mind, trust between yourself and others, and nirvana, full awakening. Nirvana literally means "blown out," like a candle flame. Free from any ties, beyond any restrictions. That's what Buddha would say is really important in life.

Part II
Cultivating Enlightened Work Relationships

When awakened by all things, the separateness of you and others drops away.

Dogen Zenji, "Genjo Koan"

"Hell is other people," wrote the French philosopher Jean Paul Sartre. He was right, but only half right. The other half is, "Heaven is other people, too." To work in an organization necessarily means working with other people—coworkers, bosses, customers, vendors, the public. Our relationships with other people are what give us most of our headaches—but these relationships can also give us much joy.

Bankers have been heard to mutter, "This would be a great place to work, if it weren't for the customers." University staff people sometimes comment, "This would be a great place to work, if it weren't for the students." Book publishers (not *ours*, of course, never never) occasionally gripe, "This would be a great place to work, if it weren't for the authors." Wherever you work, we are sure that you, too, can identify groups of people that make your life difficult. Bosses complain about their workers, workers complain about their bosses.

Isn't it funny how everyone seems to think that someone *else* is the problem? And yet, many people who work from home complain that the thing they miss the most is other people!

What are we to do? We can't seem to live with one another, but we can't live without one another. Woody Allen summarized our predicament nicely at the end of his movie *Annie Hall*, when he turned to the camera and said

> This guy goes to a psychiatrist and says, "Doc, my brother's crazy, he thinks he's a chicken." And the doctor says, "Well, why don't you turn him in?" And the guy says, "I would, but I need the eggs." Well, I guess that's pretty much how I feel about relationships. You know, they're totally irrational and crazy and absurd and . . . but I guess we keep going through it . . . because . . . most of us need the eggs.

Buddha understood this dilemma, and much of his teaching addresses how to live in community with other people. How we can work together in organizations, getting the "eggs" we all need and not hurting each other in the process. The following pages will help you accomplish this difficult goal . . . without having to walk on eggshells.

Buddha teaches that we only truly exist in our relationships. This is why their power is so great. This is why they can be heaven or hell for us. Relationships are eternal; we are not. Whether picking leaders, or building teams, or training employees, or ending conflicts, we are creating relationships, we are working through relationships. Buddha's teaching can make those relationships the path of awakening itself.

Leadership and Bosses

Lead, Follow, or Get Out of the Way

What would Buddha say about true leadership?

Bodhisattvas become chiefs, captains, priests, governors, even presidents and prime ministers. For the good of the needy they are endless sources of gifts that give rise to the mind of awakening.

Vimalakirtinirdesha Sutra 8

Buddha lived "servant leadership" long before today's business book writers and corporate consultants popularized the idea. Leadership metaphors, like management theories, come and go as fads; there's always a *program du jour* and the temptation to manage by bestseller. If you have worked in a large organization and attended a lot of training programs, perhaps you remember some of these: situational leadership, leader as coach, leader as warrior, leader as cheerleader, leader as visionary, leadership heart, leadership soul, Machiavellian leadership, leadership hardball, chainsaw leadership . . . the list is endless.

But who are the leaders we admire most? Who would we most like to follow? Moses, Muhammad, Gandhi, Jesus, the Dalai Lama . . . and Buddha. We think of them because they embody the leadership model in our quote above: servant leadership, leadership in service of the poor, the disenfranchised, the hungry, homeless and hopeless.

Leaders who serve other people are the true leaders, because their leadership goes beyond their organizations and makes a difference in the world. These leaders have given up their egos and executive trappings, and instead chosen the road of simplicity and service. What does the Dalai Lama call himself? "A simple monk." Sure, he has great power and he uses it, but he does not forget that the power belongs to the office, while the feet of clay are his own.

How would Buddha identify and select good leaders?

> *Gray hair doesn't make of you an elder.*
> *That's just age descending on you, dumbly.*
> *When gentle truth and mastery, purify and*
> *Awaken you, then you are an elder.*

Dhammapada 260–261

Age does not necessarily confer wisdom. As we all know from firsthand experience, youth ends, but immaturity can endure forever!

Good leaders are not necessarily older than their followers, but they are wiser. Leadership is not about chronology, it's about character. Buddha tells us that to be an elder, one respected in the community, one must have traveled the path of discipline, self-reflection, rigorous honesty, and self-control. To be an elder is to be a living example of that path.

Not too many years ago, a Japanese corporate executive was being interviewed by an American journalist. In the course of the conversation, the executive described his role as "being the soul of the corporation." He saw his job as being the living, breathing embodiment of the values and ethics that were the foundation of his organization. When his followers looked at him, they saw someone putting enlightenment to work.

Perhaps what many employees and organizations are yearning for today is a leader who is a Chief Spiritual Officer, not a Chief Executive Officer.

What would Buddha do about a tough, demanding boss?

See a critic as a treasure map;
Stay around and things always get better.
Let him teach and wean you from wrong action.
Good people learn to love him, others don't.

Dhammapada 76–77

Teachers who demand the most of their students help their students grow the most. It's the same with bosses. Employees rise highest when they rise under bosses who set high standards and challenging goals for them. Employees with bosses who expect mediocre performance usually give it to them. Worse yet are lax and undemanding bosses; they're doing you a real disservice by selling you short.

Buddha knows that a worker with a tough boss is like an athlete with a tough coach—that worker and that athlete will both work harder, stretch their capabilities, and reach new levels of achievement. Yes, it's hard to remember this when a tough boss pushes you out of your comfort zone, but just as Buddha says, stick with this boss, he's guiding you to treasure.

Think of your boss's criticisms and instructions as his expressions of love for you and concern for your future. As Ken Blanchard (a.k.a. "The One Minute Manager") says: "Feedback is the breakfast of champions." If your boss never tells you what you're doing wrong, how can you improve? If you're a good employee, you'll learn to love it (or at least respect it, even if you don't love it). If you're not learning this, it's time to rethink yourself, not your boss.

What would Buddha think about executive egos?

> A fool who knows he is foolish is wise in that;
> A fool who thinks he's wise fulfills the name.

Dhammapada 63

Jack Welch, well-respected CEO of General Electric for 20 years, says, "If you're not confused, you don't know what's going on." That's such a superbly Buddhist observation. Those who pretend to be masters of the situation are fooling themselves. Better to admit your unknowing. The Zen Teacher Shunryu Suzuki Roshi used to say he didn't know what he was doing, running an enormous Zen center. People thought he was being humble, but he was admitting the simple truth.

Wise people are humble people—they *know* they don't know. People with big egos are foolish people—they *don't* know they don't know. They are ignorant of their own ignorance; they are fools who think themselves wise. Thus, they are doubly foolish.

Better to be humble, like Jack Welch. If he's confused, he's acknowledging humility. He is always a beginner.

Buddha reminds us to be conscious of our own foolishness. Own and acknowledge the fact that there is much you don't know. The place of unknowing is not a bad place to be—it means you are teachable and open to learning. You can't be teachable and maintain a big ego at the same time. Suzuki Roshi wrote a lovely book, *Zen Mind, Beginner's Mind*, teaching us how to maintain the freshness of beginners. Both he and Jack Welch also retained the humbleness of beginners. Good enough for them, good enough for you.

What would Buddha do about a terrible boss?

Treating others the way he's treating me,
He'll be destroyed and then I shall be free.

Jataka 278

We hear one reassuring refrain again and again as we study Buddha's teachings: what goes around comes around. Even a bad boss will get his comeuppance. We never know in advance what the karmic punishment will look like, or when it will come, but we can rest assured that it will come. Perhaps he'll mess with the wrong employee and end up being sued. Perhaps his deeds will come to the attention of his own bosses, and they'll fire him. Perhaps his employees will unite against him and find subtle ways of turning the tables. But mainly, he will always pay the highest price: he will surround himself with dukkha, unhappiness.

The important thing here is to remember that it is not *your* job to even the score. You are not to take on the role of judge and jury with your boss, even if he's bad enough to make you want to. You stay out of his karma and just take care of your own. Do a good job at your work; be compassionate and cooperative with coworkers; try to stay out of harm's way and minimize any contact you have to have with your boss; be respectful when you do have to deal with him. This is exactly what Buddha knows and does. He doesn't soil himself with retribution, he doesn't have to.

If you *really* want to be a good student of Buddha and are willing to take on a difficult learning assignment, we have a radical suggestion: love your terrible boss. He's a nasty teacher, but he can teach you lessons your friends never can. Besides, the boss who deserves love least needs it the most.

Working with Others

Unity in Diversity

How would Buddha cultivate good working relationships?

He gives what is dear, does what is hard, bears what is painful, admits his secrets, keeps others', helps those in need, and never rejects the ruined.

Anguttara Nikaya 7.35

The path to enlightened work is definitely not the easier, softer way. Buddha knows that in order to move beyond suffering and find happiness, we must give up many of the things that at first seem most natural for us. As humans, it is our inclination to look for the easy way to do things, to hold onto things we treasure, to avoid pain, to hide our secrets from others, to gossip about other's secrets, and to avoid people who are of a lower status or those who have been ruined by some life circumstance. However, if we follow these inclinations, we will not cultivate good relationships with others at work. It really *will* be a "looking out for #1" kind of workplace, and everyone will be miserable.

If I want good relationships with my coworkers, I should follow Buddha's coaching as best I can: give to others even when I feel selfish; take on hard jobs that need doing; put up with difficult things without complaining; be honest, admit my mistakes, and ask for help; keep confidences that others share with me; help coworkers in need; and be loyal to friends who may be going through scandal or disgrace. If I want these things from others, then I must start by *giving* them first.

How would Buddha influence others?

> *He possesses wonderful eloquence for deep truths. He is extremely skilled in explaining positions and reconciling opposites. His eloquence is unstoppable; his sure intellect irresistible.*

Vimalakirtinirdesha Sutra 5

Think of someone you know at work who is very influential—someone others listen to and respect. What makes that person influential? Unless the person happens to be in the boss's family, she's influential for two reasons: competence and character.

We respect someone because she is competent, skillful in her work; she is talented, smart, well-trained, and achieves results. We also respect her because she has good character; she is honest, compassionate, hardworking, responsible, ethical, takes initiative, and is a good person.

To be really influential, you must have both competence and character. You must know your own job and do it well; and you must be a person of integrity and good character. And to tie it all together, if you can develop the ability to be consistently articulate, there will be absolutely no stopping you in your career! Your influence will be irresistible.

If you're not as articulate as you'd like to be, perhaps now's the time to sign up for Toastmasters (or in this case, Taoistmasters).

What would Buddha think about doing something extra for others?

Giving is the highest expression of the goodwill of the powerful. Even dust, if given in naive ignorance, is a good gift. Because its effect is so great, no gift given in good faith to a worthy recipient is small.

Jatakamala 3.23

Buddha taught, on a profound level, what we've all heard for years: "It's the thought that counts." Mind matters. A generous mind always finds something to give.

Smart bosses know that appreciation is what really motivates employees. The gift of a smile, or a few well-spoken words of praise in public, or a small token of recognition can go a long way to making people feel cared for and acknowledged. More substantial gifts can also be very effective when given in good faith. But be careful; small gifts and trinkets often backfire because they seem condescending and superficial. Gifts must be meaningful to the recipient if they are to be effective. Otherwise, employees see right through them.

Smart employees know that they, too, have the power of giving. Doing a little something extra for the customer engenders loyalty and generates repeat and referral business. Doing something extra for a co-worker is a way of investing in the "interpersonal bank," so that when you need a favor, you have goodwill to draw on. Giving gifts of attention, concern, and interest are powerful ways to build relationships with one another, and "going the extra mile" builds trust, teamwork, and strong morale.

You'd be surprised how simple and easy this is. There are thousands of ways to do a little something extra for others:

- Bring in some flowers from your home garden and give them to someone

- Ask what you can do to help if a coworker seems stressed or frantic

- Give your boss an article that you think would interest him, especially if there's a good chance he hasn't seen it already

- Throw in a little something extra when a customer makes a big purchase

- Throw in a little something extra when a customer has a problem

- Offer to stay late to help meet an important deadline

- Ask about coworkers' families—show that you care about them as people

- Get involved in company-sponsored activities and programs, like Junior Achievement, United Way, blood drives, local Boys and Girls clubs, etc.

- Homebaked goods are a tasty way of saying "thanks for your help"

Doing something extra is always good. It not only helps others, it's great for your karma!

What would Buddha do about a double standard between ourselves and others?

Other's faults and errors are so plain,
But our own are difficult to see.

Dhammapada 252

Have you ever noticed the double standard we use when we're evaluating someone else's behavior versus our own? Oh yeah, you've noticed it when others employ it! But here is why you don't see it in yourself: we judge ourselves by our *intentions*, while we judge others by their *behavior*. Not fair! And Buddha warns us against it, just as Jesus did (see Matthew 7:3).

Think about it. This is why we're so quick to judge other people's faults and errors: it's so easy to see them. We give them no credit at all for good intentions, because we cannot read their minds. But when it comes to our own behavior, we know we meant well and we reward ourselves for it. "That wasn't my intention; I didn't *mean* for that to happen." We try to conceal our mistakes with purity of purpose, and we expect others to understand and forgive us.

Yet again, this arises from the delusion that people are separate from one another, when in actuality we are all connected and interrelated. If we ever reach the day when we *get it* that we're not separate, the double standard will disappear. Until that day, Buddha suggests we lighten up and give others the benefit of the doubt for their good intentions.

What would Buddha say about listening?

The unlistening one grows like a bull.
His muscles swell, but not his brain or wisdom.

Dhammapada 152

"God gave us two ears and only one mouth; we should use them in that proportion." Many successful leaders repeat this, and their success testifies to the truth of the saying.

The single most underdeveloped and underutilized skill in organizations of all types and all sizes is the skill of listening. It is amazing how much you can learn, how smart you can become, simply by *listening*. Buddha tells us that we don't become wise by talking; we become wise by listening. Do you think Buddha spent his years leading to enlightenment talking or listening?

Listening individually, you learn from others. Listening in groups, when the whole group listens attentively, we learn even more. For example, in Native American–based council practices (where participants commit to always listen as others speak, and thus cannot pre-think their own words) we learn about others, we learn about ourselves, and we learn who we are together as a group. Real listening frees us to learn in these new ways. Remarkable.

What would Buddha do if someone gave him constructive feedback or criticism?

When I receive productive words, unsought,
That counsel me in useful, skillful ways,
I should gratefully accept them, always
Looking out to learn from everyone.

Bodhicharyavatara 5.74

If there is one thing most of us hate, it is unsolicited advice or criticism. It hurts our feelings; we're not prepared to hear it; we didn't ask for anyone's feedback; and we bristle with resentment. Such amazing negativity—even anger—bubbles up! But this defensiveness makes it hard for us to learn from the un-asked-for counsel.

The great and compassionate scholar Shantideva here urges you to let go of your ego and recognize the value of listening to other people's feedback, perhaps especially when you didn't ask for it. If you give in to resentment, you learn from no one. If you are grateful, you learn from everyone. If you truly want to be wise, you will view everyone as your teacher. And the most important lessons you need to learn may come from very unlikely sources. Listen carefully when someone gives you an admonition: it may be the Buddha talking to you.

What would Buddha do when teaching or training a coworker?

> *I shouldn't point the road with just a finger,*
> *But instead, using a respectful*
> *Gesture, stretching out my proper arm,*
> *I should indicate the path ahead.*

Bodhicharyavatara 5.94

The most important thing to keep in mind when training or teaching someone else is respect. Above all, you must respect the learner and honor the fact that she is where she is on her own spiritual path. If you would teach her, you must meet her where she is. Then invite her to travel further down the path by learning what you are offering to teach. Do not tell her what to do—rather, invite her to do what you are suggesting.

Every learner has the power to agree or to refuse to learn. The teacher cannot control her. The wise teacher or boss recognizes this, and honors the learner's choice. If you want to help others travel the road of enlightened work, *invite* them—don't *tell* them. This path is sometimes hard to travel. Honor it by showing a little energy yourself; and honor the learner by always showing her respect.

When would Buddha criticize someone?

In criticizing, the teacher is hoping to teach. That's all.

Zen Teacher Bankei

Bankei had trained for years to cultivate his Buddha mind, and of course he was a teacher himself. He knew both how hard it is to change and how hard it is to help another change. He knew that in this process there are times when criticism is necessary, and here he tells how to give it. His teaching is so simple, but so powerful.

When criticizing another, the teacher always hopes to teach. That's it. The teacher never criticizes to make a point, to show off his wit, or to establish his own superiority. He criticizes only to teach. If you cannot maintain the mind of teaching when criticizing, you should not criticize.

When you feel an impulse to criticize, ask yourself, "Am I about to teach something? Am I free of all other motives other than teaching?" You could be teaching the person you are criticizing, or someone else who needs to learn, and you should always be teaching yourself, learning from your actions. But unless your answer is an honest and immediate "Yes, the critique is simply to teach," hold your tongue.

Of course, this whole discussion implies that the person on the receiving end of your criticism is open and receptive to it. Do not overlook this. Do not assume that everyone is interested in learning from your insight and comments. Do not just assume the role of teacher with everyone you know, let alone the role of critic. This is especially true of your coworkers and bosses. If you are a supervisor or manager, it is your job to criticize your employees if that will help them improve. But with everyone else, it is a good idea to ask them first: "I have some observations that might help you. Would you like some feedback?" If they say "yes," you can criticize them and help them learn. If they say "no," forget it.

How would Buddha encourage people to be personally accountable?

Don't look at others' wrongs, done or undone.
See what you, yourself, have done or not.

Dhammapada 50

If there's one thing Buddha is good at, it's teaching us that we're responsible for our own lives. In every situation, we can choose to play the role of victim and blame others, or we can own the problem and thereby take responsibility for the solution.

Buddha is very wise to emphasize how we're powerlessness to change other people. In fact, we can barely change ourselves! It does no good to focus on others' shortcomings and faults, when we aren't in a position to do anything about them. Let's not be distracted; for most of us, there is plenty of work to be done in respect to ourselves.

Best to sweep our own side of the street, and let others deal with theirs. Being personally accountable yourself is the best way to set the example and encourage others to follow suit. That's what Buddha did. He lived his life in full accountability, and eventually was completely surrounded by others who lived the same way.

Dealing with Difficult People

Seeing All Beings as Buddha

How would Buddha deal with jerks?

> *As a result of our own lies and gossip we face bad*
> *workers and mean people. Whether it's our students, our*
> *helpers, or our employees, they argue with us. They*
> *disagree without even paying attention to us. They*
> *pretend not to understand until we repeat things two or*
> *three times; then they get angry with our tone and talk*
> *back and take their own sweet time to do the work.*
> *When they finally finish, they don't get around to telling*
> *us and they continue to be spiteful and angry.*

Dzogchen Kunzan Lama 83

How does this horrible situation happen to us? Why is the world so unfair?

Buddha's answer turns the tables on you. You want to know the reason everyone is treating you so badly? It's because you started it long before. Everyone knows "what goes around comes around." This saying doesn't just apply to others, it applies to *you*. It was your own hostility, your own duplicity, that began the cycle that led to your current situation. (We know . . . this isn't the answer you wanted to hear.)

Perhaps you don't even remember how it began. Perhaps you think you never treated these people badly. Perhaps you are even right about that. But can you honestly say that you've never lied in a work situation? Can you claim you have never gossiped about someone and said things that were hurtful? We didn't think so. There are no innocents among us. People are jerks to us because at some time or other we have been jerks to others. Other people are simply mirrors of ourselves.

Okay, so Buddha tells you why you're faced with these bad relationships. Now what to do about them? It is very simple and also very difficult. You began this cycle of negativity, you are going to have to end it. When faced with meanness, be compassionate. When you encounter inattention, zero in on what those people are really thinking. When you wait through delays, maintain mindfulness of your inner reactions. When you receive no thanks, remember your reward is in this valuable lesson.

This is a difficult path to walk; we understand, we've walked it ourselves. But it doesn't last forever, and by following it you may dramatically change your future path. Don't give in to your anger or that of others, just keep your mouth shut and do the right thing. That is the bodhisattva path.

What would Buddha do about coworkers who lie?

Animals express their true feelings in their cries.
Only humans are smart enough to hide the truth.

Jatakamala 22.19

The human capacity for self-awareness is both our blessing and our curse. We feel, yet we have the capacity to stand outside ourselves, to feel ourselves feeling something, and to choose whether or not to let others know. In other words, we always have the choice to express our thoughts and feelings or to express something different.

This ability to dissemble causes a lot of trouble at work. People lie at work when they feel they must hide the truth. They may think if they disagree with the boss, it will hurt their careers. If they point out the weakness in a business idea, they'll be branded as "not team players." Such beliefs teach us to lie. We end up with whole organizations full of people lying to one another. Hard to be enlightened and awake if you have to lie about what you see and think.

Buddha would be compassionate about all this lying. He knows co-workers who lie are not bad people, they have just lived in an environment of lying for so long that they're blind to how much it harms them. Buddha would encourage leaders to transform their organizations by rewarding people for telling the truth, no matter how bitter, and by not rewarding lies, no matter how sweet. He would tell workers not to sell their integrity for a paycheck. No paycheck is worth that price. Buddha would invite all of us to emulate the clarity of animals—to say what we mean and mean what we say.

What would Buddha do about people who fail to practice what they preach?

Reciting prayers but flouting their commands,
He's like a cowboy counting others' cattle.

Dhammapada 19

Disdain for people who do not practice what they preach is nothing new in organizational life, or life in general, as the above quote demonstrates. Some 25 centuries ago, Buddha saw people going through the motions, failing to "walk their talk."

So, what to do about it? We don't need to do anything about it. A person who is "all hat and no cattle" (as they say in Texas) will reap his reward: zero. Some people fail to live up to their talk because the cattle aren't theirs, so they can't be bothered. Some people simply find it easier not to follow through.

Don't worry about their reasons. Just make sure you are walking *your* own talk! If you are vigilant about making sure that your words and deeds are always in alignment, your integrity will be intact and you'll realize you always have something at stake: your life.

What would Buddha do if someone badmouthed him?

> *A bad person who slanders a good one is like a person who looks up and spits at heaven. His spit never reaches the sky; it falls back into his own face.*

Sutra of Forty-two Sections 8

When you're getting trashed by someone, it is often hard to remember that, in the long run, this is going to come back and hurt the person doing the trashing. Buddha helps you keep the proper perspective. Perhaps you wish the trash-talker would get his comeuppance as fast as the person who spits at heaven. Stop wasting your time with these thoughts.

Buddha's simile tells us another crucial thing about this situation. When you are badmouthed, you are like heaven in the simile. Does heaven spit back at the badmouther? No. It is the badmouther's own bile that comes back at him. It is the same when someone badmouths you. Do not respond in kind. Do not sink to that level. Let gravity simply take its course and the bad words find their way home. No effort is required; this is just the way of things.

Buddha is in a good position to know this—he was constantly getting slandered by jealous religious figures. He just let it be. Things turned out pretty well for him, didn't they? (And, hey, you don't have to rise to the celestial purity of Buddha; you just have to stay out of spitting range.)

What would Buddha do about people who hurt him?

"He insulted me, he beat me, robbed me!"
Think this way and hatred never ends.
"He insulted me, he beat me, robbed me!"
Give this up and in you hatred ends.
Not by hate is hate defeated; hate is
Quenched by love. This is eternal law.

Dhammapada 3–5

Conflict is a fact of organizational life. Following their desires and attachments, people are bound to hurt one another in the course of working together. But conflict's naturalness doesn't mean that we should let it continue

So how should we handle workplace hurts and conflicts? We naturally want to respond in kind when others are hostile toward us, but Buddha tells us to resist this inclination. Other people's hostility often has nothing to do with us—they are just acting out their own karma. If we meet others' anger with our own anger, joining in their negative karma, we are simply adding fuel to the fire, endangering everyone, including ourselves.

Instead, Buddha counsels us to take the high road—to respond to others' hostility with compassion and forgiveness. Wise teachers throughout the ages have echoed Buddha's wisdom: Jesus, Gandhi, Martin Luther King, Jr., and so many others in other cultures. The soothing balm of unconditional love and understanding is the only thing that calms hostility in others.

Is this a tall order? Of course it is. We are human, after all, and Buddha knows this. But harboring a resentment because someone else hurt us is like swallowing poison and hoping the other person will die. And acting vengefully, taking an eye for an eye, only leads us to the kingdom of the blind. We must forgive and let go of revenge—otherwise we become prisoners of our own anger. Quench your hate in the waters of love. It's a slow business, but a sweet one.

What would Buddha do about adulterous affairs at work?

Four things for one who beds another's wife:
Loss, unrest, censure, and finally hell.

Dhammapada 309

Buddha would say the same thing about sexual affairs whether they are at work or someplace else: adulterous affairs are costly to the illicit lovers. The text above outlines what will happen to the male partner, but we can safely assume that a similar price will be paid by the female partner.

First, the lovers will immediately feel degraded and will lose the respect of those who know about the affair. Second, the lovers will lose sleep because of their guilty consciences and their worry about being found out by their spouses and everyone else. Third, the lovers may very well be censured. It is not uncommon that one partner or the other may be forced to resign their job, if the affair becomes a matter of public knowledge and the boss (or the human resources department) finds out about it. Adulterous affairs are costly to an organization in terms of gossip, morale, attention, and productivity, and smart managers and executives act quickly to discipline the illicit lovers.

Finally, the lovers will pay the price of hell. Not necessarily hell of the fire and brimstone kind, ruled by the red guy with tail and horns, but the hell of being trapped by desire, attachment, deception, lying, broken vows, and more. Hell is where we live when we spite the path of awakening, and choose instead to be slaves to our desires.

Buddha would mince no words in counseling the lovers about the high cost of their adulterous affair. His own censure would be compassionate, but there's not much he can do to save these people from the results of their own actions.

What would Buddha do about self-righteous "experts"?

An educated man who, with his learning,
despises one who never went to school
Is just like a blind man in the dark,
Carrying around a lamp he cannot see.

Theragatha 1026

Don't you just love the imagery here? Buddha has a great sense of humor in describing the arrogance of fools. He is quick to burst the bubble of ego wherever he sees it, for he knows that ego is the antithesis of enlightened work. The intellectually benighted are the truly blind. Buddha had no patience for them at all.

Sometimes the person with the least education has some of the best ideas at work. Education, with its emphasis on the "right" answer, can stifle people's curiosity and creativity, creating an educated boor. If you think you already know everything, there is no room for you to learn anything. As Jesus said: who has eyes, let them see. It doesn't take a degree to light a lamp; it just takes using your eyes.

What would Buddha do about whiners and negative people at work?

Don't stay with friends who cheat or do what's base.
Stay with noble friends; stay with the best.

Dhammapada 78

Buddha doesn't mince words with his advice: avoid whiners, chronic complainers, and any other negative people. Avoid them like the plague. Why? Because it's contagious. Just as a drunk wants you drunk, too, if you're going to be around him, so whiners want you to join in their whining. It's easy to get sucked into the negative energy of negative people— we all have frustrations and complaints about work, and sometimes it even seems like fun to join in the pile-on of cynicism and anger. But don't do it. Resist the pack mentality that transforms these negative people into jackals. Run away if you must.

Instead, seek out positive people at work. Look for people who are up to something good and hang out with them. Make a list of the five or ten most-admired people where you work and see if you can find ways to spend some time with them. Remember: they, too, want to spend time with sincere people; that means you. At the very least, watch them and see what you can learn from them.

Associate with honest people, good people, people who are good at their jobs. If you really want a good future, hang out with the best. Why? Because that's contagious too.

What would Buddha do if he had a conflict with a teammate?

> *When conflict arises in your own family, don't blame others. Instead, look for the cause in your own mind and action and pursue the solution there.*

Anguttara Nikaya 3.31

Peace within a team, like peace within a family, is vital to the well-being of both individuals and the group. Blaming someone else does no good at all—in fact, it makes things worse. If you think the problem lies in someone else, then the solution must lie there as well. There's nothing you can do; you're powerless. This is no way to be. Instead, if *you* own the problem, then you begin to own the solution. You will think of things you can do to make things better (no matter what the other person is doing).

When team conflict arises, ask yourself: "How have I contributed to this situation?" You know it takes two to tango; it's doubtful that you are ever simply an innocent victim. (And if somehow you *are* an innocent victim, drop that role now. Own the problem and empower yourself to end it.) Look for what you can do to contribute to a solution. Victims assign blame, winners make things better. In the end, would you rather be the one who's morally right, or the one who's fixed the problem? (Hint: which one do you think your company prefers?)

Customers: Love 'em or Lose 'em

Customer Service as Bodhisattva Practice

What would Buddha teach about the importance of customer service?

> *May I be, in many ways, a support for all the living beings throughout space, for as long as all are not yet satisfied!*

Bodhicharyavatara 3.22

Buddha taught that serving others is our true work, no matter what kind of job we may happen to have. For it is through serving others that we overcome our own natural self-centeredness. This the true work of the whole world, for in this work we all escape *dukkha* (suffering) together. As long as we are focused on ourselves, we continue to feel the pull of desires and attachments; but when we turn our attention to the needs of others, we find happiness and we're freed from our own endless wanting.

Today Buddha would tell us that customer service people are the most important people in our organization. If the organization exists to serve the needs of clients or customers (and why else would an organization exist?), its most important members must be those who most directly serve them. This remains true whether you work for a money-making business, a non-profit group, or a government agency. Customer service is the purest kind of Right Livelihood. And Right Livelihood is central to Buddha's path.

Serving others transforms your organization while it transforms the world. If you can take a cranky, unhappy customer and solve his problem, you will transform him into a loyal customer. He, in turn, will tell others about how you helped him, and they will come to you, too. And, if you treat them well, they will tell still others, and the word will spread quickly, building your business for you, while you simply serve people's needs.

Consider how Nordstrom has established a new paradigm for the world of retail, simply by serving superbly, consistently. Consider how Disney has transformed the world of family entertainment, with its theme parks, movies, television programming, and retail stores. Consider how Southwest Airlines has set a new standard for the world of air travel, with their unique style of delivering the basics. Everyone in those organizations has just one job: service excellence. If every business and organization took serving others as its number one job, the world would indeed be transformed—and so would their bottom lines!

What would Buddha tell customer service people?

It is quite clear that everyone needs peace of mind. The question, then, is how to achieve it. Through anger we cannot; through kindness, through love, through compassion, we can achieve one individual's peace of mind.

The Dalai Lama, *The Dalai Lama: A Policy of Kindness*, **p.51**

Buddha knows customer service is hard work. Customer service is hard because it's so easy to let the negativity of others break down our own moods, our own mind. Buddha would remind customer service people of the compassionate core of Buddhism and of ourselves. In customer service, our job is to give peace of mind to our customers. We *must* do that through kindness and compassion.

Enlightened work is just ordinary work done with an enlightened mind. Nowhere is this more true than in customer service, where you are serving people, helping them solve their problems, taking care of their needs. Here, attitude is everything. You may try to take care of your customers with a mind that is bored, distracted, or resentful; but you will become unhappy and so will they. Take care of your customers with an attitude of service. You will feel fulfilled in your work, and your customers will be satisfied too. If you truly do this, the individual who gets peace of mind can be the customer—and can be you as well.

What if you don't feel so great or you are having a bad day? Buddha would say, "*Act* your way to a positive mind." Try transforming your unpleasant feelings through pleasant actions. The shortest path is through service. Making your customer's day will make yours.

What would Buddha do to handle an angry customer?

> *The insults you offer me, though I don't insult you;*
> *the taunts you throw at me, though I don't taunt you;*
> *the berating you give me, though I don't berate you;*
> *all of that I do not take from you. It's all yours, sir.*
> *It's all yours!*

Samyutta Nikaya 7.2

Buddha understands that a customer's anger is not personal, even though it is directed at you and might seem personal. An angry customer is really angry at the situation; you just happen to be the person getting talked to, so naturally you get the anger. In this case, Buddha emulates the animal realm: he lets the anger roll off his back the way beads of water roll off a duck. It's not your anger, you don't have to take it. What a relief!

At the same time, Buddha would not let the customer's *problem* roll off his back. Buddha's life purpose was to help others, so he would immediately do whatever he could to help the customer. Buddhism is very practical on this level, emphasizing doing the work of the moment.

While Buddha did not have customers in the sense that our businesses and organizations have today, as head of a large institution, Buddha did listen to complaints and respond to them. We can use his guidance to create a list of some suggestions Buddha might make for handling an angry customer:

- First, be compassionate. The customer is frustrated, angry, disappointed, and upset. Do not meet anger with anger. Meet anger with compassion. This is good exercise for you on your own journey.

- Thank the customer for bringing his problem to you. Your mission in enlightened work is service, and you cannot be of service if there are no problems to fix. The customer has brought you a gift, an opportunity to help him. Treat his complaint as the gift it genuinely is.

- Listen carefully to what the customer is telling you. As you listen, sift through the words and sort out facts from feelings. You must deal with both facts and feelings if you want to make the customer happy again. Responding to just one side is not enough.

- Take notes, if it is appropriate, explaining that you want to make sure you have the information correct so you can help.

- Emphasize what you *can* do, not what you cannot do. Point out what is possible, not what is impossible. The customer has had plenty of experience with negatives; work from the positives.

- Get help from others if you need it. You may need the assistance of another department, or a coworker, or your boss. This might even be emotional assistance, a chance for a breather. This is okay.

- Explain and educate the customer as you continue to interact with him. You may be able to teach him things that will enable him to prevent this problem in the future. This is a blessing you give to the entire world.

- Commit to what you can do. Be clear about what the customer can expect and when. Be modest in your commitment; do not commit to something you are uncertain you can deliver. Always best to under-promise and over-deliver, if you can.

- Thank the customer again for the opportunity he gave you to serve him.

- Follow up. Keep your commitment; do what you said you would do; and keep the customer informed if anything changes.

And remember, problems may be solved but they are always replaced. They're endless. In the final analysis, your process is your real work.

What would Buddha say about bad customer service?

Aware of the suffering caused by exploitation, social injustice, stealing, and oppression, I vow to cultivate loving-kindness and learn ways to work for the well-being of people, animals, plants, and minerals . . .

The Second Precept as recited by the Tiep Hien Order

Despite the myriad books and seminars on customer service, it seems that many individuals and organizations still don't get it. In fact, sometimes it seems as if customer service is getting worse, not better! Why is this so, and what would Buddha suggest we do about it?

Buddha would remind us that most human beings are operating out of ignorance (along with greed and hatred—the three poisons). They don't see the true nature of things, especially themselves. Their faulty perception leads them to think they are separate from everyone else and need to survive—even if it means screwing someone else. When people are in "survival mode," they will use any means necessary to survive, including exploitation, prejudice, stealing, and oppression. Exactly what the Second Precept calls us to beware of.

Businesses are just like people when it comes to survival. They'll do the same things, and they'll encourage employees to do them as well. Not only will they be duplicitous in their relationships with competitors, they will even act this way with their customers! This is why we find people who lie to make a sale, warranties riddled with loopholes, business scams, shoddy merchandise, knock-off imitations sold as genuine, poor-quality workmanship, deceptive advertising, and so on. Survival-at-any-cost thinking comes with terrible social costs, here and (saddest of all) in developing countries. The personal price is no picnic, either.

Only by seeing the other as the self can we escape from this cycle of abuse. So, only by seeing the customer as the company can we create a new cycle where both of them respect and please one another. To use a relevant Buddhist metaphor, we are as interconnected as the parts of a car; only when working together do the tires, the frame, the seats, the engine, the steering wheel have meaning and function. Without that interrelation, there is no car at all. Our customers need us and we need them, just as do the parts of the car. The answer to bad customer service—and bad business in general—is awakening to the vital nature of our interdependence.

Part III
Creating an Enlightened Workplace

What makes you think work and meditation are two different things?

Akong Tulku Rinpoche, *Enlightened Management*, p.3

Who *wouldn't* want to work in an enlightened workplace? A place where people work hard and feel good about it; a place where trust is high between management and employees; a place of honest, open communication; a place characterized by integrity, personal responsibility, mutual respect, high achievement, personal satisfaction, joy, and great results—isn't that where *everyone* wants to work?

Well, of course—but where does such a place exist, this Pure Land for workers? No need to call a headhunter, scan the want ads, or send out dozens of résumés, in hopes of finding an enlightened workplace. It isn't *out there*, it's *in here*. It exists where people want it to exist, and are willing to work together in creating it for themselves.

How do you start? Start where you are. There is a haunting Zen story of a monk who asks how to enter his path toward enlightenment. His teacher says, "Do you hear the sound of the stream? Enter there." How? It's not a question of *how*, it's a question of *now*.

If you're a manager, supervisor, or executive, you can start by thoroughly assessing your leadership practices, the example you set for others, and the way you manage your people to get the job done. Start where you are.

If you're a non-management employee, start by looking at how you do your own work, how you interact with coworkers and bosses, and especially how you handle problems. Again, start where you are. *Everyone* has a role to play in creating an enlightened workplace.

From humble beginnings grow changes that shape organizations. When Buddha's spirit animates the day-to-day activity of the workplace, the organization inevitably begins to wake up. This is what we mean by enlightened work. And an organization where enlightened work is getting done begins to change the world. Work is not a value-free zone; it is a profoundly powerful place to change the world.

Some of the ideas in this section should open your eyes to where to turn your attention first. Don't wait for someone else to start creating the enlightenment; you may have a very long wait. It is vital that you start. Now.

The Big Issues

Beyond the Bottom Line

What would Buddha do to become a great employer or boss?

> *A good employer ministers to her servants and employees in five ways: by assigning them work they can manage; by giving them food and money; by supporting them in sickness; by sharing special delicacies; and by granting them leave when appropriate.*

Digha Nikaya 31

Buddha knew that no matter what kind of an organization you run, it is smart to be as good an employer as you can. When there's plenty of labor, the best and the brightest will want to work for you. And when there's a shortage of labor, you will still be able to choose the best and retain them.

Being a great employer is not some mysterious, complex thing; it's about getting the basics right. Buddha lists five:

1. Assign work that employees can manage. Make sure job requirements are a good fit with employees' skills and abilities; make sure they have appropriate education and training. Also build enough challenge into each job to maintain employees' interest. This may be difficult to do with some jobs, but give it some thought and be resourceful. Things like cross training, job enrichment, job enlargement, job rotation, and special projects can all help keep your people challenged, engaged and committed over time.

2. Give employees food and money. Larger employers provide company cafeterias and smaller ones have lunch rooms with

refrigerators and microwaves. Productivity and health are directly related. You must pay employees well and care for them well if you expect them to care for you and their work. Nothing is more important.

3. Support employees in sickness. Everyone gets sick once in a while; and when people are sick they need special care. If you give them that care, they will gratefully return it many times over when they return to the job. In today's medicalized world this is expensive, as Buddha knows. But he is crystal clear: provide healthcare for your employees.

4. Share special delicacies. A little extra something every so often is a wonderful way to let people know you appreciate them and their good work; sharing the goodies, whether profits or in some other form, is highly reinforcing.

5. Grant employees leave when appropriate. People are not cogs in a machine and cannot be treated as such. Special circumstances require benevolence and flexibility in allowing time away from work, whether for maternity leave, family care, a sabbatical to "recharge the batteries," or other personal needs. When that recharged worker comes back, new ideas will more than make up for lost time.

What does it take to be a great boss or employer? Buddha has laid out the basics. By all means, add to this list, but don't miss the boat by missing the basics.

What would Buddha say about making a profit?

> Beginning with only a little cash,
> The wise can skillfully cause it to grow,
> Like the slowly building wind can cause
> A spark to grow into a mighty fire.

Jataka 4

People often imagine Buddha as an other-worldly ascetic who thinks we should renounce money and the material world. It is true that Buddha did this, but he hardly expected everyone to do the same. He didn't want the world to fall apart. He was very much in favor of making a profit, provided that it was done in keeping with the basic principles of awakening: honesty, integrity, personal responsibility, right livelihood, cooperation, harmony, and so on. In fact, making a profit with enlightened business practices would be a perfect example of Buddhism in action. Remember, the dharma is, above all, practical, teaching us how to live and work in the real world. You can't get more real than the world of work.

Buddha points out that it doesn't take much to start a successful business. You can start small and build. How many hundreds of companies started on the kitchen table or in the garage of an entrepreneur with a good idea? From humble beginnings, great enterprises grow. The wise person, one who follows Buddha's teachings about skillful practice, can build the business slowly, steadily, as one would build a fire. By all means, get a nice little blaze of profit building there. You can toast some mighty tasty marshmallows over such a fire.

What would Buddha consider when writing a mission statement?

I am not satisfied simply doing hard work and carrying out the affairs of state. I believe my real duty is the welfare of the whole world, and doing hard work and carrying out the affairs of state are just its foundation.

King Ashoka's Sixth Rock Edict

King Ashoka was perhaps the greatest Buddhist ruler in history. He established a dynasty in India, over two thousand years ago. He began with force but he converted to Buddhism and changed his mission. He saw there was no point in ruling over a great kingdom that did not serve the people. He realized his real duty—his dharma, which means his truth as well as his job description—went beyond strengthening the government; it went even beyond his country. His dharma was to provide a vision of welfare for all the world. That is why, though his dynasty has vanished, his values continue to work for the welfare of the whole world.

Heading a company is like this. In the final analysis, our business mission is not merely to work hard and carry out business affairs. These are only the means of achieving our real mission, which should always be the welfare of the whole world. Of course, like Ashoka, we need to take care of the foundation; we can't build without a foundation. But a foundation is pointless unless we build something real and lasting on it. Visionary business people know this; they feel the deep need for this; they feel this as their dharma. And they give the world innovations that better our lives.

"But what if I'm not the CEO?" you ask, "What if I'm just someone who goes to work every day?" You may not be able to change the company's business goals or the welfare of the world, but you can change the goals of your own working group. Think about the welfare of your group. What would add to it? What trouble is it having? Your work environment is a little world, one you spend a good deal of your life in. Everyone in it should be working for its welfare. This is your dharma, to make a world worth being in every day.

What would Buddha think about contemporary business language?

We do not become noble doing harm;
We gain this name by being kind to all.

Dhammapada 270

The biblical book of John opens: "In the beginning was the Word."
Yes, language is powerful; without our even noticing, words shape how
we think and how we act. Current business language shows how at
odds many of our organizations are with the fundamental teachings
of Buddha.

"We're going to crush our competition." "Business is war." "It's a
dog-eat-dog world." "Learn how to swim with the sharks." "Leadership
secrets of Attila the Hun." "Chain of command." "He's getting his march-
ing orders." Business language is so often military language, sports
language—adversarial, win/lose—ultimately about hurting or destroy-
ing other people or organizations.

What would Buddha make of this? He would say it reflects our
erroneous thinking that we are separate beings. He would remind us of
our interconnectedness, that when we hurt another living thing (and
organizations are living things, made of people), we hurt ourselves as
well. For Buddha, business language should reflect the Buddhist aim to
be noble. We are not noble when we "eliminate the competition." We
are noble when we do no harm. So be conscious of the words you use.
Buddha made Right Speech part of the Eightfold Path. Enlightenment
begins with the Word.

What would Buddha do about investing in the future?

A treasure stored in a deep pit makes no profit and is easily lost. Real treasure is gathered through charity, piety, moderation, self-control, and good deeds. It is securely kept and cannot be lost.

Vinaya Mahavagga 4

Looking at these words philosophically, we can see the echo of Jesus's words in the Bible: the true treasure is love, not gold. Buddha knew this too, and we all know this deep inside ourselves.

We can also look at these words as an endorsement of values-based business practices. Buddha is clearly in favor of the idea of making a profit, but he encourages us to make our profit in the right way, with solid values and ethical behavior. Warren Buffett (a billionaire with values) and many other successful business leaders today would concur with Buddha.

An enterprise that hoards all its resources greedily will soon find itself with no public goodwill, no partners with other businesses, and employees who feel disheartened and exploited. On the other hand, an enterprise that builds partnerships with other businesses, treats employees as valued partners in the business, sees itself as a responsible member of the surrounding community, and shares its resources with the poor and needy, will be an organization that is built to last. Customers will be loyal, as will employees. The "treasure" of goodwill will be there in good times and in bad. Buddha knows that an enterprise such as this understands that "doing well" and "doing good" go hand in hand.

How would Buddha develop
a learning organization?

With work comes wisdom; without work, no wisdom.
Know the path and work to increase wisdom.

Dhammapada 282

If Buddha were around today, he would likely use a vivid metaphor to
bring the importance of continuous growth and learning to life. "Consider the shark," Buddha might say, "who must constantly move forward
or die. He must keep moving through the water, so that the water will
move through him, bringing him oxygen, keeping him alive. So too does
your organization need to keep moving, or it will die. Learning is endless, and the more you know, the more you realize how much you don't
know. The moment your organization ceases to be a learning organization, in that moment it begins to die."

We should conduct ourselves so that wisdom will grow. Our organization's structures should be designed to facilitate learning at all levels,
in all areas, even if at first we don't see the relevance. Our policies and
procedures should be written and implemented to encourage continuous
learning, even though this might upset our schedules. Our work spaces
should be arranged so that we can easily get together and learn from one
another. And organizational leaders must lead the way, always themselves learning and developing their wisdom.

What would Buddha do about corporate philanthropy?

A bodhisattva does not give food and drink to gluttons and drunkards. . . . And though it's his own wealth, if those he's responsible for are distressed when he gives it away, he doesn't do it.

The Precious Jewel of the Teaching 12, quoting the Ratnavali

How much should a business leader give to charity? A significant chunk? A token amount? Here the Buddhist teachings remind us that a business leader's best contribution may be putting money back into the company. After all, charity begins at home. When Bill Gates and Ted Turner gave away billions of dollars, some criticized them for neglecting their primary obligation to their own companies and the wealth those companies could create for their shareholders. Did they go against Buddha's teaching?

Buddha says two wise things about giving: First, one should never give money or things to those who would misuse them. We know this already, but it is sometimes hard to resist such giving, since people may clamor loudly for our gift, or may try to induce guilt if we resist. But we must be firm in our resolve. Giving must go to those who will use the gift well. There are so many worthwhile, deserving recipients to choose from today, that we must make sure we do not squander our generosity by giving poorly.

The text gives us another wise word: One must be careful not to harm one's own company in one's charity. After all, it is employees who actually generate the wealth through their hard work, and it is shareholders who invest their money in the company's future. It is inappropriate to be generous with outsiders if one has not first been generous with insiders. Certainly, if it harms employees or the health of the organization (even indirectly, through employee resentment or shareholder bad feelings), one should not give away wealth no matter how worthy the recipient.

Giving is a fundamental virtue, but we must think of the larger picture when we give. Does the recipient really gain? Will others be inadvertently be hurt in the process? The answers are not always easy, this is why we must ask the questions.

What would Buddha say about responsibility for the environment?

When you throw away your spit and toothbrushes,
You must hide them well away from sight.
Dumping waste in places that we share
And in the water system leads to ill.

Bodhicharyavatara 5.91

For Buddha it's just as true at work as at home: we must treat the places we share with respect, and with six billion people on the planet, *every* place is a place we share.

For instance, your organization's policies on paper recycling have the power to go far beyond your company's walls, because they actually create public perceptions and markets. This is especially true if you work for a large corporation. When a few large companies make the change to recycling paper and to buying recycled paper even for reports, proposals, and correspondence, many other companies will take notice. When many companies make this change they will create a market that will change the economics of scale in recycled paper and drive the price down. Finally, we'll all be so comfortable with recycled paper, we'll wonder why people ever wanted paper bleached to blinding whiteness. Then we'll be able to follow Buddha's words and stop dumping dioxin into the water system.

This is how change happens. It might start with one person within the company who keeps bringing up recycling at meetings until something gets done. Corporate responsibility does not necessarily start at the top. It can start with anyone who has the courage, patience, and persistence to be a voice of integrity and to keep speaking until others take up the chorus and join you.

How would Buddha hold onto capital?

When a family can hold onto its capital for a long time, it is always due to one of four reasons. They always search for what has been lost. They repair what is old or broken. They are moderate in eating and drinking. And they always put a good person with principles in any position of authority.

Anguttara Nikaya 4.255

Despite the dangers of money for our selfish selves, Buddha recognizes that capital is absolutely necessary for any group. He lists four ways a family holds onto capital, and these work just as well for an organization.

The first two rules are closely related. Never abandon what has been and can still be useful. If it's lost, go find it. If it's broken, go fix it. Our mania for newness (the new new thing!) in business is both wasteful and unsustainable. For example, take the corporate habit of replacing office furniture and decor wholesale. If we bought solid, well-made desks and covered the floors with genuine wood, or high quality carpet, we wouldn't have to change them so often. And if we had those genuine wood things, we could repair them instead of throwing them out. This is real cost-cutting, spending a lot on a desk that lasts a hundred years, not buying "bargain" furniture every time the company reorganizes or wants to change its image.

And we could apply this lesson to people as well: Employees should never be thrown away, but rather selected and hired carefully, as long-term investments, and treated accordingly, with ongoing training, coaching and development of skills. People should be cared for and cultivated for best long-term results, not seen as disposable commodities, to be dumped at the first sign of tough times.

Translating the third rule to an organization, it means being moderate in consuming resources. It means recycling and buying recycled supplies. It means flying coach. It means helping teamwork by sharing spaces. It means no fancy executive dining room. There are a thousand such ways to save.

Finally, an organization always has to lead by example. Anyone in authority must be principled and fundamentally a virtuous person. Notice Buddha does not say "smart" or "decisive" or "charismatic." These things are optional; virtue is not. Without virtue as their foundation, no amount of intelligence, hard work, or charm will make up for the lack of confidence the people will feel in their leaders. Real success depends on real character.

Work Practices and Processes

Practice Is Awakening

What would Buddha counsel about short-term versus long-term thinking?

> *The farmer ploughs and plants his field well. But a farmer has no magic power to command "Today let my crops sprout up. Tomorrow let the grains come forth. The day after let them ripen." No, only time can make this happen.*

Anguttara Nikaya 3.91

Most Eastern cultures traditionally take a much longer view of time than Western cultures. These views are rooted in religion. Buddha shared the Indian long-term perspective on time. He understood that character development is a life-long process (or even longer!), and that patience and persistence are its keys. This is also true of many aspects of organizational life. We are often planting seeds whose fruits lie months or years away.

Everything has a season—so we read in the remarkably Buddhist book of Ecclesiastes, in the Bible. You cannot control the seasons, nor can you rush them. And so it is at work. Some work activities yield results quickly, while others are long-term endeavors. Both are important, but if there is an area where most of us are lacking, it is in long-term thinking. Many of us want instant gratification; we want to see results right away. We dig up our carrots every week to see if they are growing. We are an impatient lot.

Buddha counsels us to develop patience; it is one of the Ten Perfections Mahayana Buddhists strive to embody. Learn to trust that all endeavors yield appropriate fruits in their own time. Notice we didn't say "your time," but theirs.

How would Buddha design work processes?

> *Gathering reeds and branches and binding them into a raft, he crosses to the safety of the other shore, depending on the raft and the effort of his hands and feet. Having crossed over, he thinks, "How useful this raft has been! . . . Why don't I carry it on my back as I go where I want?" What do you think, monks: in doing this, is the man doing the right thing with the raft?*

Majjhima Nikaya 22

Buddha knows how easily we humans become attached. We become attached to all kinds of things, including the work processes we're familiar with. If something has worked for us in the past (the raft) we cling to it long after it becomes a burden. Often we're not even aware that we don't need it anymore. We fall into habit, doing things the way we have always done them. It is comfortable, familiar, and easy.

In business this is an especially tricky problem if we have been successful, but don't know exactly why. Jim Shaffer, a senior newspaper executive, calls this "superstitious learning"—fearing that if we change anything, we will screw up our successes. For instance: a baseball player wears his lucky socks; a performer has her little pre-performance ritual; a student transcribes her notes in her special notebook, in order to maintain her straight-A average. If something has worked for us in the past, we are loathe to let go of it even if we *know* we don't need it now. We might need it again in the future; hey, that future could be now; letting go of it might *create* the dreaded need for it; oh yeah, we had best hold onto it. Ah, attachment, the root of all suffering.

Buddha is consistent in his teachings: let it all go. Everything is changing—always has been, always will be. Continually look at your work processes in light of today's work, not yesterday's. If you are still holding onto processes that add no value, then you are burdening yourself (and your organization) uselessly. Be awake: when you've reached land, drop the raft. Overhaul your work processes as often as necessary to stay current.

What would Buddha do with technology?

Before you start and after you finish working, make this one simple gesture toward your computer: Give it a nod . . .

Some people might balk at the idea of showing respect to a machine. Doesn't that imply subservience, they ask?

Besides, the machine acts so impetuously, who can respect it? Why show respect to something so arbitrary and unreliable?

Because it gives to us.

Philip Toshio Sudo, *Zen Computer*, p.40–41

Buddha would welcome any technology that improves our lives. Like any tool—a hammer, a chemical, a knife—a tool is not good or bad in and of itself. It is just a tool, an object we can use for good or bad purposes. If it does good things, Buddha welcomes it. So Buddha would support ongoing technological development.

When we show respect for people, they are more likely to live up to it. They are also likely to respect us in return. Perhaps it is also so with computers and other forms of technology: when we respect them and treat them well, they are more likely to work well for us. They even seem more likely to respect us.

Our computers may not have minds (though there are days when we swear they *do* have minds—evil ones), but they are indeed slowly progressing toward consciousness. For now, when we treat them with respect for how they improve our lives, we begin to create a reality where they *do* improve our lives.

Respect does not imply subservience: respect implies an affirmation of goodness. If a technology gives to us, let us acknowledge and encourage it. This will help us control the technology mindfully and keep doing good with it. If we bow to our meditation cushions (and Buddhists do), we surely can bow to our computers.

What would Buddha think about the internet?

The Web site you seek
cannot be located, but
endless others exist.

Anonymous haiku, found on the Internet

Buddha would profoundly appreciate the infinite world of cyberspace, and its endless possibilities. He would see in it a reflection of the infinite universe around us: vast, complex, marvelous to behold, each tiny piece of the great Web potentially linked to every other. Disordered, ceaselessly changing, vulnerable to attack, finally indestructible, the Web indeed reflects our world.

So Buddha would caution us: just as we can never satisfy our endless desire for worldly pleasures, so we can never satisfy the our endless desire for virtual pleasures. The Web site you seek cannot be located. You can use your senses to search for pleasure or you can use search engines, but your satisfaction will only come when you search within and find no one to satisfy. Luckily, though the Web site cannot be located, neither can the user.

What would Buddha do about telecommuting?

Followers might be thousands of miles away, but if they remember the precepts, they will surely gain the fruits of the path. But if those right next to me forget the precepts, they might see me every day, but they will not gain the path.

Sutra of Forty-two Sections 37

Many managers today are still reluctant to let their people work from home. "How do I know they're working if I can't see them?" they ask. Buddha would reply, "How do you know they're working even if you *can* see them?"

Looking busy is not difficult for most employees. Many organizations mistake "face time" (the amount of time each day when the boss and others can see you at work) for hard work and productivity, when in reality face time is simply face time. You may see me at my desk, or in my work area, but how do you know what I am really doing? I might *look* busy, but am I busy doing company business, or am I busy doing personal stuff?

Buddha understood it's not physical proximity that makes the difference between a good employee and a bad one, it's the quality of the employee that makes the difference. An employee of intelligence and integrity will work hard no matter where she is working—in the office, on the road, or in her home.

What would Buddha do? Select and hire the right employees, train them, then trust them to do a good job and reward them for doing their work well. Good employees remember the precepts wherever they are.

In real estate, the key is location, location, location. In business, the key is good work, good work, good work. Don't confuse the two.

What would Buddha think about business gurus and consultants?

> *Whether you're looking inside or outside, whatever you find, you've got to destroy it. If you find a Buddha, kill the Buddha.*

The Record of Lin-chi 19

What's the definition of a consultant? A consultant is one who borrows your watch and then tells you what time it is. Buddha would like this definition. He would tell you to "kill" the consultants—not literally, of course (by the way, please don't literally kill Buddhas you meet, either) but kill off the awe and reverence with which you slavishly follow them. Buddha did not have a Harvard Ph.D., nor did he wear pinstripe suits, or carry a business card from McKinsey. And even if he did, as a genuine Buddha, he would tell you to think for yourself.

Yes, you might need some help, someone to be a resource for you in solving problems, exploring alternatives, and creating new opportunities. But don't ever let someone else tell you how to run your department or your organization. A good consultant is like a doctor: he can diagnose your problems, he can assess your strengths, and he can provide you with information and resources to help you get better. But ultimately *you* are the one who is going to eat healthy foods, do the physical therapy, get rest, take the right medicines at the right time, and mobilize your resources to get healthy. *You* are the one who's going to do the work and do the healing. No one can do it for you, even if he does have a bestselling business book on the *NY Times* list. So don't hang onto authority, even Buddha's. Let go and keep moving.

What would Buddha do to improve communication within an organization?

> *He speaks when it's appropriate, with truth, wisdom, and restraint. He speaks only when it's right, and speaks only what is profitable, well-supported, clear and effective.*

Anguttara Nikaya 10.176

Buddha was clear about the difference between good communication and bad communication. Bad communication is gossip, idle chatter, saying hurtful things to someone or about someone. Individuals should exercise self-restraint and good judgment in how they communicate with one another. Likewise, an organization would do well to engage in communication that is profitable, well-supported, clear and effective.

Communication seems like such a simple thing on the surface, yet most organizations can't seem to do it well. Consider: when asked how they would prefer to get their information, the overwhelming majority of employees report they want it directly from their immediate boss. Their second preferred choice of information is team meetings. But when asked how they actually *do* receive most of their information, employees report their number one source is the company "grapevine" (gossip), and second is written memos—the least preferred sources!

Buddha would make leaders talk directly to employees. That is what he did and he mandated in his own organization. Buddha would start some good ol' face-to-face conversation, either one-on-one or in groups. He would warn us to resist the urge to communicate important information on a mass scale, either through company-wide emails, memos, or newsletters. As a rule, with communication, the more impersonal, the less effective. Buddha was clearly a hi-touch kind of guy, not hi-tech. Email, faxes, memos, and bulletin boards all have their place, of course, but Buddha knew that there was something special about the personal touch. He knew that nothing beats clear, effective, honest communication between human beings.

So if you want to improve communication where you work, start by having honest, clear conversations with those around you. Who knows? You might start a communication revolution in your organization. All revolutions start somewhere.

How would Buddha run an effective meeting?

First, the passion for analysis and knowing defiles the Buddha Nature. Second, the passion for emotions and desires defiles the Buddha Nature.

The Lion's Roar of Queen Shrimala 3

Everyone knows that meetings get bogged down in many ways. A group meeting is a lot like the human mind, filled with conflicting desires, energy and impulses, short-term and long-term goals, digressions and distractions. What covers up the mind's original purity is not so different from what covers up the original purity of a well-intentioned meeting. Two distinct types of passions derail meetings: the passion for analysis and the passion for emotions.

The passion for analysis and knowing is commonly referred to as "analysis paralysis" and is familiar to anyone who has worked in a large organization. But even small groups of people can fall victim to this passion. Analysis and knowledge are somewhat deceptive, because on the surface they make it look as if something is happening and the group is doing its work. Yet if you watch carefully over time, you will see that a group overcome with this passion is simply going in circles, unproductively rehashing the same material, searching in vain for reassurance that a mistake will not be made and that success is a sure thing. Once on this track, the more analysis, the less clarity the group has. The group debates and analyzes for so long that the window of opportunity for action closes, and it becomes too late to do anything. The group has analyzed itself right into inaction.

Other meetings become ineffective through the passion for emotion. People in the grip of this passion desire an intensity of emotion that will empower the group, but they allow what begins as rational debate to escalate into irrational argument. All ability for good judgment can be lost, and discussion of issues and facts devolves into personal attack. Passions run high, tempers flare, people say harsh things they will regret later, and the group spins out of control into conflict and chaos. The final result is either inaction or wrong action taken in the heat of the moment.

Buddha tells us to beware of both too much rational analysis and too much irrational emotion. Both are extremes that lead to bad ends. Remember, Buddha teaches us the Middle Way, a way in which we balance reason with feelings, rationality with intuition. We can avoid the extremes by staying present with what is going on in the moment, and bringing ourselves, and our meetings, back to awareness and choice.

Care and Feeding of Employees

Your Team as Your *Sangha*

How would Buddha select and hire the right person for the job?

> Until you've come to know the spiritual state of living beings, don't assume anything about the shape of their abilities. Do not wound the healthy. Do not force those wishing to walk the wide world onto a narrow path. Do not try to pour the deep ocean into cow's hoof-print . . . Do not confuse the glow of a glowworm for the light of the sun. And do not force those who love the roar of a lion to listen to the cry of a jackal!
>
> **Vimalakirtinirdesha Sutra 3**

Appearances can be very deceiving, especially when it comes to human beings! Buddha is saying here that unless you've done the work hiring takes, you just might judge a book by its cover. Big mistake.

Most organizations waste enormous amounts of time, money, and energy cleaning up the mistakes they have made by hiring people without due diligence. Far too many managers still hire on the basis of "a gut feeling." Most people make hiring decisions based on who they like and who they feel comfortable with. Far too little attention is paid to checking out the job applicant's work history, skill level, ability to learn and grow, and most important, ability to work well with other people.

It is common knowledge that people get hired for their technical skills; they get promoted for innovation; and they get fired for their trouble with interpersonal skills. Fully 80% of people who fail on the job fail because of poor interpersonal skills. They just don't get along with their coworkers, boss, customers, or all of the above.

So how would Buddha select and hire the right person for the job? Buddha didn't exactly hire people—he attracted followers, people who wanted to learn from him and follow his example. So our recruiting differs from Buddha's, but understanding Buddha's teachings can still give us some idea of how he might go about hiring, if he were working in an organization today.

Buddha would begin *inside*, using his mind to clarify what kind of person he was looking for and wanted to attract. He would include both character and competence in his thinking. He would set the stage to attract someone with good values and integrity, someone who was walking his own spiritual path. And he would create an environment that would attract someone who has the necessary skills to do the job, or who can learn those skills.

Secondly, Buddha would tap into all we have learned through human resources research on job success factors—he would take advantage of the experience and wisdom of those who have studied job applicants and their performance track records. Buddha was methodical, not a man driven by whim and impulse. He would do his homework and approach the job of hiring in a methodical way. Here are some of the steps he might advise us to take:

Make sure you have a good pool of applicants by casting your net as widely as possible. Don't limit your search to obvious candidates.

Be clear on what you want. Think through exactly what is required in the job. Make a list of the duties and tasks. Make a list of the results you want achieved. Make a list of the personal characteristics you're looking for.

Consider what it takes to be successful in your particular organization and/or department. Think about people who are successful and list the behaviors and character traits that make them successful. The new person coming in doesn't just have to be a good match for the job, she has to be a good match for your organizational culture.

Involve many people in the interview process. Others will see things that you will miss or overlook.

Ask behavioral questions. The best predictor of future performance is past performance. Ask tough questions: "Describe a time when you had to deal with a difficult customer. How did you do it?" "Tell me about an instance in which you made a serious mistake. How did you fix it?" "Tell me about a time when you had to handle a conflict with your boss. What did you do?" Questions like these get at real-life behavior and uncover the candidate's real values and character.

Experts in selection tell us that hypothetical questions are practically useless. Anyone can make up an easy answer to a question like "How would you handle a supply-side problem?" People spin nice stories when they project themselves into hypothetical situations; these future projections rarely predict how people will actually behave.

Make sure the candidate, too, has an opportunity to ask lots of questions. Hiring should be a two-way process. Here is an opportunity to practice active listening. You can learn as much about a candidate from questions she asks as you can from the answers she gives.

Don't be in a hurry to hire. Haste in the beginning can be costly later on, when you begin to see what you missed.

Use job tests wherever you can, whether it's a typing test, a computer simulation, a role-playing scenario, or some other kind of test designed to really bring out the skills and abilities required to do the job.

In addition to looking at a candidate's past performance, be sure to consider her future potential. Ask about generic skills that can transfer from job to job: budget skills, organizing, solving problems, writing, making presentations, coming up with new ideas, cutting costs, working well with others, and so on. The candidate may not have done the particular job you are interviewing her for, but if she has the right generic skills, she can easily grow into the job and do it successfully. Smart employers hire with an eye to the candidate's future potential, not just her past experience.

Be sure you are honest with the candidate about the nature of the job as well as future growth potential. You don't want to misrepresent a job to the candidate and have her quit in disappointment when she discovers the truth. A good candidate is interviewing you as you interview her; you need to act with the honesty you demand.

Finally, look especially carefully at someone who "interviews well" or tries to get away with glib answers to questions. She may be skilled at interviewing, but make sure she also has the other skills to back up her brilliant interviews. Do your homework on the candidate: listen carefully, watch how she behaves when she is nervous, ask tough questions, be patient, and work to discern her true character.

Yes, all this is time-consuming. But you can either put in the time on the front end of the relationship or you'll spend the time later dealing with discipline, coaching, re-training, even firing and re-hiring. You choose where you'd rather put your time.

How would Buddha advise training departments?

Do not think that I intended to create a "teaching system" to help people learn the way. Do not hold such a view. What I teach is the truth I have found. A "teaching system" means nothing because truth can't be divided into pieces and rearranged in a system.

Diamond Sutra 6

Again and again Buddha resists our efforts to pin him or his teaching down into a neat little system. He knows how much we long for security and reassurance in a world that is constantly changing. We want him to give us those "Seven Easy Steps to Enlightenment," or "The Ten Top Ways to Get Nirvana Now." Just check out the bestseller lists today—the books we buy speak volumes (and volumes and volumes) about how we humans think. We love those books that promise us a wonderful life by following X number of steps, tips, or checklists. Even Buddhism has plenty of lists, but Buddha never tells us that learning the way and walking it is easy as checking off a list.

Instead, Buddha says that teachers must *resist* the urge to try to boil things down to recipes. Trainers must not make false promises by oversimplifying the complexity of business. Learning can never be systematic, because each person learns differently. Each person must experiment, make mistakes, struggle, ask questions, explore alternatives, and find his or her own way on the path to enlightened work.

Buddha stayed with his students to help them find their paths. Nowadays, teachers can't usually do this, so they need to create a learning environment—one in which people are challenged, with problems to solve and goals to accomplish, in collaboration with others. Everything at work can be part of the enlightenment process. Former President Ronald Reagan once said, "The best training program is a job." Buddha would agree.

What would Buddha do to increase employee morale?

> *Get rid of your selfish mind and create a mind sincerely focused on others. Making someone happy inspires that someone to make someone else happy. In this way happiness spreads from one act.*
>
> *One candle can light a myriad of others and continue to shine just as long as before. Sharing happiness never decreases it.*
>
> **Sutra of Forty-two Sections 10**

In this lovely passage Buddha explains the basic and beautiful truth of happiness, a truth as basic to making employees happy as it is to making all living things happy.

Paradoxically, the more we work at gaining happiness, the less likely we are to experience it. Happiness doesn't come from "looking out for number one." Happiness doesn't come from "what's in it for me?"

So how do we increase employee morale and make our people happier? Look at what Buddha did. He didn't call for more company picnics or feel-good T-shirts for everyone. Nor did he send out for pizza on Fridays. Instead, he just lived with his community; he went on alms rounds right along with the newest monk; he encouraged them with his example and with his constant presence. He shared what he had, his own happiness, and he never ran out.

Buddha's example and presence taught even the lowliest monk that if he wanted to improve his morale, he could start where he was, by looking around for someone to share with. So if you're in that position, help someone who has something to learn or has fallen behind. It is not your complaints about morale that will improve it. Don't curse the darkness— light another's candle.

What would Buddha teach about job security?

Being a collection of its fingers,
A hand is not an independent thing.
The same with fingers, which are made of joints.
And those joints, too, consist of smaller parts.
These parts are then divided into atoms,
And atoms split in various directions.
At last these fragments collapse into nothing.
All are empty, lacking real existence.

Bodhicharyavatara 9.85–86

We would like to have job security. We would like to have security in general. This is natural, but it's also unrealistic. In our economy, most people have long since given up the expectation of spending our whole working life with one organization. But many people still lament the passing of "the good ol' days" when employees were loyal to their organizations, and vice versa. But those good ol' days were merely a blip in the overall history of work. If you look back over the many thousand years of human history, the notion of job security is a very recent thing, occurring only in the past 100 years or less. The expectation of "job security" was a new phenomenon, brought about by the development of modern capitalism, the industrial revolution, unprecedented job choice, and the human mind's desire for permanence and stability.

In the last two decades, we have learned that job security breaks down when companies break down. Buddha reminds us that companies always break down, like all things. We like to think of our organizations as real and solid, especially when we're counting on working there for a while. But organizations are only as solid as their structures.

And structures are only as solid as their employees. And employees are only as solid as their minds and bodies. And as we have all experienced, both bodies and minds change over time.

Look what the Bodhicharyavatara is saying about our bodies. They are made up of many parts, like feet and hands. But hands are made up of fingers, and fingers of joints, and joints of still smaller parts down to atoms and electrons and quarks and other particles that only last the briefest moment and die away. Where is the solidity in all this? Buddha tells us it is simply nowhere. Permanence and solidity do not exist and never will.

Today we see that job security was an illusion all along—a shared myth born of desire and circumstances. We have awakened from our illusion. There is no job security and there never was. Our only job security is our ability to secure a job. Work with that.

What would Buddha do to guide career development?

> *Engineers work water; fletchers arrows.*
> *Builders master wood; the wise their selves.*

Dhammapada 80

The world is full of rich natural resources that best meet human needs with a bit of shaping and guidance. Engineers work water into canals so water can work for us. Fletchers make arrows for food and protection. Builders cut and carve wood into furniture and housing, to help us live more comfortable lives. All of them manage and use natural resources for our ends.

So who guides the natural resource of humanity? Buddha says that *we* do. There is no one outside us to shape us into better humans—we must do that ourselves. Like engineers, we must channel our own energy. Like fletchers, we must sharpen our skills with precision. Like carpenters, we must smooth our minds to enjoy peace and comfort. We have the raw material of our lives with which to work, and we are responsible for what we create from that material.

This means we are also responsible for our own development as employees. We should not look for someone else to hone our skills and develop our raw talent for us. We each must do that for ourselves. A fool sits and waits, saying, "Here I am, boss. Teach me something and make of me what you will." The wise person takes the initiative and says, "Here are my career goals, these are my talents and abilities, and this is the kind of training I think I need to accomplish my goals. Can I count on your support?" The wise master themselves.

Solving People Problems

There Are No Answers—
Pursue Them Lovingly

What would Buddha do about policies and procedures?

Where is
The list
Of things
To not
Worship?

Lawson Fusao Inada, "The List"

Most organizations' official policies and procedures are another example of our inclination to try controlling life, to make it predictable, manageable, consistent, and fair. As if demanding order is enough to create it!

While the intention to create order is not always bad, it is impossible to implement consistently. New situations and problems always arise, and we have not yet thought of rules for them. So we make more rules. We manufacture elaborate formulas and detailed explanations to make our rules precise. We publish big, fat policy manuals, so everyone will know what the rules are (though few will read them), and our work world will be as safe, orderly, and well-organized as possible. Our policies and procedures give us an answer for every eventuality . . . well, almost. We keep adding more rules, but we never delete any of the old ones. We begin to worship our policies and procedures; they become sacred texts.

This happened even to Buddha's organization, the *sangha*. During Buddha's life they developed an elaborate system of rules, responding to everyday situations. Just before Buddha died, he told the monks they could get rid of all but the few major rules. Trouble was, they couldn't discern which ones were major and which were minor, so the book of rules has grown amazingly rigid and indeed become a sacred text. This is *not* what Buddha wanted.

Buddha knew that rules often hurt us. We lose track of the *spirit* of the policy, and we get bogged down in the *letter* of the policy. We become ensnared in bureaucratic minutiae, tangled up and tied down in heavy cobwebs spun by busy spiders in pinstripe suits. We become paralyzed, losing the efficiency the rules were designed to protect.

There are few organizations that understand this problem better than Nordstrom, the department store chain, world-renowned for their superb customer service and excellent people practices. Nordstrom's employee policy manual has just one page and one rule:

> Rule #1: Use your good judgment in all situations.
> There will be no additional rules.

Buddha would smile.

So, what would Buddha do about policies and procedures today? If he worked anyplace other than Nordstrom, he might take the pages of his company policy manual and use it to line the bottom of a songbird's cage. When the pages were finally all gone, he would open the cage and set the songbird free.

What would Buddha do about compensation and employee benefits?

Calling yourself a bodhisattva yet ignoring others and going a different way is totally absurd. It's like killing your child and then treasuring his effects.

The Precious Jewel of the Teaching 10

If we are going to earn the name of bodhisattva, a person who truly works for the good of all living things, then we cannot ignore the needs of others. In fact, they must be our foremost concern. We cannot say one thing and do another. The classic Tibetan text we quote here expresses this powerfully. And the metaphor it uses clarifies the importance of compensation and employee benefits.

To apply this quote, we should see the business owner or manager in the position of the parent. The parent's duty is to respond to the needs of the child, or in this case, the worker. This text warns us against setting up the wrong values and somehow caring more for the child's effects than the child when she was alive. The child is what matters.

The same applies to workers. The leaders of every organization say, "Our people are our most important asset." And yet, if we look at the internal practices of many of these organizations, reality often does not match their rhetoric. An elite few at the top reap the rewards of the work of everyone else, and the gap between executive compensation and average workers continues to grow obscenely wider. Training is viewed as a benefit or a perk, not as an investment. Employee benefits fall far short of employees' real needs. Cost-cutting often leads to corporate anorexia. Despite what their leaders say in public, too many organizations value profits over people.

In contrast, Buddha says an organization's leaders must respond to the real needs of the workers. If people truly are your most important resource, *everything* in the organization should reflect that, including compensation, benefits packages, rewards and recognition, management practices, training, job titles, the sharing of space and resources, scheduling, opportunities for advancement and promotion, and much, much more.

What would Buddha advise about diversity issues?

> *Just as the Buddha-lands are diverse in their qualities but without difference like the sky, so the awakened ones are diverse in their bodies but without difference in their understanding.*

Vimalakirtinirdesha Sutra 11

Diversity is a paradoxical subject for Buddha, since at the deepest level there *is* no real diversity. Diversity implies separation of essentially separate things, but when we get down to the (non-)essence of things, there is no separation—we are all not-two.

But of course, when we look around at other people, we *perceive* diversity—diversity of skin color, body shapes, age, sexual orientation, personality, work style, values, thinking patterns, skills, talents, and so on. It looks to us like people are very different from one another, on many different levels. Since we must live on this practical level, what should we do about diversity?

The teaching above makes the path clear. We should acknowledge and appreciate our human differences, and recognize the need for "different strokes for different folks." Buddhism has always celebrated the diversity of people, awakened ones included. It can do this because it recognizes their fundamental unity. In fact, you can follow Buddhism and another religion *at the same time.* In Asia, many Buddhists are also Confucians, or Taoists, or Bon-po worshippers, or followers of a whole tapestry of different local religions. Buddhism has always adapted to the diversity of the cultures it has spread to. It's doing that in North

America, too—in this book, for example. Buddhism, more than any other world religion, embraces diversity.

As Buddhism embraces diversity in lands and people, so it embraces diversity in the workplace. Jobs, work space, communication, work schedules, employee benefits, incentives, work styles, preferred type of leadership, etc., all should adapt to the diversity of people and cultures. We must not insist on one-size-fits-all practices, for to do so would dishonor the diversity that makes things work.

The paradox is that, at a deeper level, we are all the same. We support diversity because we know that we are fundamentally so alike. We all want a fair day's pay for our work; we want appreciation and acknowledgement of our contributions; we want respect; we want interesting, meaningful work; we want to make enough money to meet our living expenses; we want kindness and compassion from others; we want to feel good about what we do for a living; and so on.

The challenge of diversity from Buddha's perspective is to do justice to both our differences *and* our fundamental oneness. If we treat everyone exactly the same, we dishonor human diversity and uniqueness. If we treat everyone differently, how do we maintain equity and fairness?

Let us suggest the family model, for an organization is in many ways like a family. When a family includes several children, parents know that each child needs somewhat different parenting since each child is unique. But parents know that they also have to be fair in treating each child equitably. Parents will tell you this is not easy. In fact, it is very hard. It requires constant awareness of the developmental needs of each child, balanced against the needs of the other children, and constant vigilance to maintain time, energy, discipline, attention, and love in the right proportion in each situation. This also involves frequent negotiation with the children themselves. Everyone, both parents and children, has a part to play in maintaining equity and fairness within the family.

So it is in the workplace. Everyone, both management and rank-and-file, has a role to play in creating a diversity-friendly, enlightened organization. This requires constant communication, frequent negotiation and re-negotiation, flexibility, willingness to change, and above all, compassion and humility. Is it easy? No. Is it worth it? Buddha says yes.

What would Buddha do about stereotyping?

> *. . . all women appear in the form of women, but they*
> *appear in the form of women without being women.*

Vimalakirtinirdesha Sutra 7

This is another version of "You can't judge a book by its cover." The sutra explains forms as artificial constructs, delusions based on our inclination to categorize people and miss their deeper Buddha nature. As humans, we are so quick to assign labels to other people: woman, man, black, white, Asian, Hispanic, old, young, straight, gay, white collar, blue collar, pink collar, management, employee, and many, many more labels. In labeling others, we think they are separate from us, that they are "other" than us. With our stereotypes, we totally miss the point that we are all not-two; we are all interconnected and interrelated, as the individual fingers on a hand.

If we have *any* essence, it's the Buddha nature; the path of enlightenment simply shows us how to wake up to that fact. Until we wake up, we label others as inferior because we are not yet aware of our own Buddha nature, and by extension, everyone's Buddha nature.

Bottom line: those who must stereotype others deserve compassion the least, but need it the most. They are asleep, bound up in desire and attachment, driven by fear and anger, much in need of enlightenment— just like ourselves, but more so. Indeed, sexists and racists appear in their forms without being those forms. Free yourself through freeing them from themselves.

What would Buddha do about sexism?

You may want something, or you may be unhappy, but if you don't let this lead you off into thinking "It's like this because I'm only a woman." . . . Then you yourself are Buddha.

Zen Teacher Bankei

Bankei doesn't mince words; he says as long as a woman doesn't feel her gender limits her, then she's already Buddha. If she's Buddha, well, we reckon she can be anything she wants to be in the workplace. So here is the first lesson on sexism: the Buddha in you is not sexist and does not respect sexism or any other kind of prejudice. Do not sell yourself or anyone else short on account of gender.

Here is another lesson, a history lesson this time. The historical Buddha lived in a tremendously sexist culture, 2500 years ago. Being a product of that culture, he was not bias-free; he believed an order of nuns would shorten the authority of Buddhism. But he admitted that women could become Buddhas, so he let them be nuns. We estimate in these actions he was about 2450 years ahead of his time. If that leaves him fifty years behind our time, that's still a great record. Let's all strive to be 2450 years ahead of our time. Do you think women will be fully recognized as equal 2450 years from now? Then do what Buddha would do and start acting on that today.

Here is lesson number three. Bankei moved forward from the historical Buddha's position. The best forms of the Buddhist tradition are constantly evolving, growing, bettering themselves. Just like the woman in Bankei's sermon, they are not trapped by their problems because they are not trapped by their self-definitions. This is the model for all of us, no matter our gender. Do not be fettered by your own self-limiting beliefs. Even if you're a mere man, you're still a Buddha.

What would Buddha do about sexual harassment?

People who can't get enough fame, money, and sex are like a children licking honey off a knifeblade.

Sutra of Forty-two Sections 22

Buddha was clear about the kind of trouble we get ourselves into when we pursue our appetites and desires to excess. Yes, needs for peer recognition, money, and sex are normal, but they're also insatiable. If we chase after them, we're asking for trouble. It makes no difference if you are lusting after fame, wealth, or sex; they are all desires and they all cut like knives.

Experts on sexual harassment agree, sexual harassment is almost never about sex at all; it's about power and domination. A sexual aggressor in the workplace is trying to demonstrate that he (94% of sexual harassment is initiated by men) is the "alpha male" who can have his pick of the females. This is basic animal behavior. Perhaps the sex is nice, but the game is really about who's in charge.

So what does Buddha teach about the lust for power and control? Like all external prizes, you may win it, but it is only a matter of time before someone bigger and stronger than you takes over and becomes the new "top dog." Your lust will remain, but your fulfillment will not.

On the practical level, what do we think Buddha would do about sexual harassment if he were working in modern organization? Looking back to his teachings, here is the application to this onerous problem:

First, Buddha would look at himself and make sure his own behavior was above reproach. Right Speech and Right Action are central to the path.

If Buddha were a boss, he would teach his employees about sexual harassment laws—both the spirit of the laws and the letter of the laws. Those laws are based on respect for all individuals and the right of people to feel safe where they work (Buddha would refer to it as the well-being of all people.) He would teach not merely the law, but the morality of human relationships on which the law is based.

And Buddha would stop harassment of any type if he saw it going on around him, whether he were a boss or simply one of the workers. He understood that the welfare of individuals is dependent on the welfare of the whole group. Everyone has a stake in maintaining a harassment-free environment, because any harassment affects all workers.

How would Buddha mediate between squabbling coworkers?

I will not be brought down by the fighting
Of childish people in their little quarrels.
Their words arise from conflict and emotion.
Instead, I'll understand and give them love.

Bodhicharyavatara 5.56

Buddha is, above all, compassionate. He does not judge the squabblers as bad people, but simply recognizes them as squabblers. They are where they are on their own paths. We can't get discouraged, depressed, or angered when our coworkers are quarreling, anymore than we get when we see children arguing on the playground. Since it's in our nature to fight, many of us will fight. We need to strive to see that these fights are as ephemeral as playground tiffs.

Buddha tells us to understand this fact and to act lovingly. We must listen to both sides, soothing hurt feelings with patient words, helping the coworkers find options or compromises they all can live with. Buddha tells us to be peacemakers, working with compassion and understanding to help others mature. Note that this does *not* mean necessarily making them happy; it means making them mindful of the other's conflicts as well as their own.

What would Buddha do if he had to fire someone for poor performance?

The Buddha performs acts that discipline, because he wishes to show that negative actions have consequences. . . . The monk supporting the teaching does the same. Seeing an offender or harmer of the teaching, he drives them away with censure.

Mahaparinirvana Sutra 4

Of course Buddha teaches us not to harm others, even animals, even insects, when we can help it. But this does not mean we need to let the termites eat our whole house. Some employees are like termites. They weaken the entire business, hurting other employees, and often customers too. Buddha would say that they have to go. Luckily, we don't have to kill them like termites, but sometimes we do have to fire them.

When someone needs discipline, we must provide discipline, sometimes even expulsion. This may be hard for us: hard because we may be reluctant to hurt the person, or hard because we may be angry at him and want to hurt him. Here we need to go back to the fundamentals: compassion and wisdom.

Buddha tells us to fire people, but only when their negative actions have demonstrated their impact and shown we must withhold our teaching, our company, our benefits from them. When we fire someone, we must remember why we are doing it. We fire someone because we care about every person in the workplace and every person we serve. We harm every one of them if we allow one person to undermine what we're doing, for an organization is only as strong as its weakest employee. This is wisdom. We actually harm problem persons when we don't deal with their poor performance or misconduct, for they will never learn to do better unless they experience the consequences of their own behavior. We cannot be passive here, though we act as gently as we can. This is compassion.

So Buddha would fire an employee reluctantly, but confidently, because he would do it for the greater good of the organization as well as of the person being fired. In his own time, Buddha was able to help even persons he disciplined. From our childhood on, we learn important lessons from punishment—when it comes from a place of wisdom and compassion. This is why many learned powerful lessons from Buddha's punishments and why they might learn even from yours. We may not always be successful in teaching good lessons when we fire people, but we must keep from teaching bad ones.

Buddha's situation was obviously different from ours today. He had followers who joined him in order to learn from him—they did not come together to make a product or provide a service. We can, though, still take Buddha's lessons on justice, compassion, and community and figure out for ourselves how Buddha might accomplish the difficult job of firing someone. Given what we know about Buddha, he might do something like the following:

First, Buddha would ensure that the person had been given every opportunity to succeed in his job; that he had been given appropriate training, coaching, and loving support all along the way; and that he was not simply thrown into a job to sink or swim on his own. Firing should never be the conclusion of a flawed process.

Second, Buddha would ensure that the person had been given an opportunity to improve his performance, once it became clear that he was not living up to expectations. The person should have had several respectful, concerned warnings that there was a problem, and been provided with support in trying to improve performance.

If the person was still not performing up to standards and all fairness and patience had been extended to the person, Buddha would clearly and compassionately tell him he was being fired, and facilitate a departure that was quick and clean.

Buddha would not lie to the fired person, or to others, about the nature of the firing. For not only can that person learn much from these consequences—others can also learn from seeing that poor performance has consequences. Everyone in the organization has a stake in understanding that good performance will be rewarded, and poor performance will be punished. Fairness and equity are important components of building trust in management and trust in an organization's practices. Just as democratic countries have open judicial systems, where all citizens can see for themselves whether the punishment suits the crime, we also need to have open systems in our companies and organizations so we can see that rewards and punishments are fair, just and loving.

Above all, Buddha would make sure at every step of this process that his heart was free from malice or revenge. Instead, his heart would be filled with loving-kindness (albeit "tough love") for the person he was firing, for his other employees, and for everyone else with a stake in his organization.

Organizational Problems and Solutions

If There Is **No Solution,**
There Is **No Problem—Only Mind**

What would Buddha do about the rat race of work?

Snared by desire, we hop like hares in traps.
Fettered and bound, we suffer on and on.

Dhammapada 342

Lily Tomlin has said, "The problem with the rat race is that, even if you win, you're still a rat." Buddha would have appreciated that. He compared people to rabbits caught in a snare, hopping around and around, not able to free ourselves, and suffering for a long time. This is what happens when we let ourselves get seduced by the illusion of happiness presented in such things as promotions, bonuses, higher salaries, corner offices, important job titles, and other "carrots" that get dangled in front of us to induce us to do what our superiors want us to do. We get caught up by our desires—we think that the next big pay increase will make us happy, or the new job will do the trick, or even beating out the other guy for that plum assignment. But of course it doesn't make us happy, at least not for very long. Like hares in traps, we are ensnared by our own desire for the next big thing.

We can't blame it on our bosses—after all, they are chasing the carrots dangled in front of them, too. We are creatures driven by our insatiable desires, and because we know this, we design compensation systems, recognition programs, and all sort of other goodies to manipulate each other (and ourselves) into achieving the organization's goals. Think about it for just a moment. Is it not perfectly transparent? The goodies escalate to preserve the illusion that *eventually they will be enough*. But they never will be.

It's not bad to chase goals and run the maze of the rat race. It's fine to do, as long as you're aware of what you're really doing. Just don't expect the goodies to make you happy. Run the race for the joy of running.

What would Buddha do about analysis paralysis?

If you fall into even a moment's doubt, the devil enters your mind.

The Record of Lin-chi 17

Lin-chi wasn't afraid of something out of *The Exorcist*, but something much worse: inaction. (How curious that Zen is literally the "meditation" school of Buddhism, but Zen teachings always bring us back to action.) The great Chinese teacher Lin-chi may have been the most intense of all Buddhist teachers in trying to get us to snap out of it and *do* something!

It's not that you shouldn't consider your actions carefully, making sure you act in accordance with your principles. Buddhist teachers for 2500 years have been telling us that. But also, do not spend too much time thinking and worrying about what might be. If you spend too much time studying a problem, fretting about all the unknowns in the future, you will surely be undone by your own doubt and indecision.

And once you've made your choice you simply cannot look back. Do not second-guess your choice or your strength will be sapped by the devil of doubt. In the final analysis, work life is all about *action*. It is action that leads to production and services. It is action that creates new products and pleases customers.

Even mistaken actions may be better than no action, for mistakes can almost always be undone, and often much is learned from them. The desire to avoid mistakes is what lies behind analysis paralysis, but it is a misguided desire. For if you never make mistakes, it means you are not taking enough risks. And you have to take risks if you want to grow. If Buddha had spent his life playing it safe, he would never have *become* the Buddha. Playing it safe never leads to greatness.

What would Buddha do about divisiveness and factions within the organization?

Should any monk provoke a split in a united community or continue to push a divisive issue, the monks should admonish him: ". . . be reconciled with the community, because a united community, on good terms, free from infighting, repeating the same vows and rules, dwells in peace."

If the monk . . . continues, the monks are to urge him up to three times to stop. If while being urged he stops, that is good. If he does not stop, the situation requires community meetings.

Vinaya Sanghadisesa 10

Buddha and the community of monks, the *sangha*, developed these rules over time, responding to problems as they came up. This rule is one of the most important: splitting the sangha is never the right thing because a split sangha never recovers all its force or creativity. It is the same in an organization, in a department, or in a work group.

When someone is provoking divisiveness, Buddha tells us to try to get that person back in harmony with the larger group. He even tells us how to do it, for Buddha was an early teacher of conflict resolution.

First, go to the person privately to coach and counsel him; do not humiliate him in front of his coworkers. You can do this up to three times, giving stronger counseling each time.

If that fails, call the group together to meet with the person, as a form of group intervention, multiple times if necessary. Sometimes the group must take such a drastic step, in order for the troublemaker to finally recognize how his actions are hurting everyone, including himself.

The group must work together to make sure that factions or cliques do not develop, for such splintering will seriously hinder the group's work, in more ways than one.

Abandoning a person during this process is not an option, because to do so weakens the whole group. The leader and the team must make every effort to help the person mend errant ways. Only in the face of complete failure to admit culpability or reform can the leader act to cut ties with the person. In his compassion, Buddha knows we should use all our persuasive powers as peers to keep group members working cohesively together. If one member fails, the group itself has failed a little bit, too.

What would Buddha do in a corporate crisis?

Through attention, effort, and restraint,
The wise make islands floods cannot erode.

Dhammapada 25

Recent business history and today's news pages confirm the wisdom of Buddha's words. Remember how well Tylenol came through the product tampering crisis, back in 1982? The CEO took initiative instantly, pulling his products from store shelves, at enormous cost to the company. The speed and wisdom of his response to a deadly crisis insured the company would rebound, with renewed public confidence and resulting strong sales. This is how to handle a crisis effectively.

Unfortunately, we see far too many examples of how *not* to handle a crisis. Calculating damage-control and manipulating the audience is not the way. Look at some of the corporate crises of recent years: the Exxon Valdez oil spill, the nuclear accident at Chernobyl, the chemical leak at Bhopal, the discrimination suit at Texaco, scandal and corruption in various police departments, even sexual scandal in the highest office in America. When these crises hit, spin did not help. Wisdom was called for, but not forthcoming. The damage was permanent.

Crises happen to all kinds of organizations: military, government, healthcare, church, philanthropic, professional, etc. You cannot protect your organization from all crises, but you *can* help ensure that you and your organization are not destroyed by them. Think of Buddha as the first crisis management consultant, and heed his advice: through attention, effort, and restraint, you stand firm as the crisis swirls. You are ready to work again when the flood subsides.

What would Buddha do
to turn a business around?

My supernatural power and marvelous activity:
drawing water and chopping wood.

The Record of Layman P'ang

In India, holy persons are expected to perform miracles—Buddhas included. But Buddha taught his followers not to reveal any miraculous
powers in public. Why is this? Because such powers distract people
from what really matters. People get all absorbed in the supernatural
and they forget to attend to the natural, the things that form the back-
bone of life—and work. Layman P'ang shows us how Buddhism and
work are all about being there and getting it done without complica-
tions and without show.

Why do organizations fail? The reasons are varied, of course, but
often it's because they lose sight of the fundamentals. They don't get
done what they need to get done. If you're making a product, you have
to make it well and price it right. This is not so complicated. It's about
focusing your attention on the basics, just like Layman P'ang, living in
his forest hut, getting water and wood: simple and essential. The core
activities of an organization are what keep everything going and make
the organization successful. In today's language, we would say pay
attention to "where the rubber meets the road." It's the modern equiv-
alent of "drawing water and chopping wood."

Buddha would turn around a floundering business by getting back
to basics, making sure there was water and wood when needed. Even
at the top of an enormous corporation, the boss has got to remember
this. Think, for example, of Apple Computer. It was floundering in the

late '90s and given up for dead by many business analysts. The company brought back its visionary founder, Steve Jobs, to turn it around. What marvelous thing did he do first? He slashed the product line and the budget to focus on designs that worked. He got back to Apple's basic strength. Does that reveal miraculous powers? No, but it sure was miraculous for the stock price.

It is basics, always the basics, that make things run. Not necessarily core products, but core processes. Sure, there must be vision, but vision doesn't create anything without good ol' simple work. Drawing water, chopping wood.

Appendix A

Who Was Buddha?

Buddha was not born as Buddha. He was born Gautama Siddhartha, into a ruling family, the Shakya clan, in northern India around 500 B.C.E. His father created an opulent pleasure palace for him, in hopes that Siddhartha would never leave, but instead would rule after him. The boy's every wish was fulfilled, and he was protected from ever experiencing suffering, pain, or disappointment. He lived a life of luxury and indulgence. When he was old enough, he married and had a son.

But this lifestyle of the rich and famous finally began to wear on Siddhartha, whose great mind grew curious about life outside the palace walls. Legend tells us that his father allowed him to make a trip into the local town, but ordered the servants to arrange things so that Siddhartha would not see anything unpleasant or ugly on his journey. Yet (by chance?) Siddhartha saw the Four Sights: an old person, a sick person, a dead person, and a holy person.

Siddhartha was deeply troubled by the first three sights, and asked his servant if aging, sickness, and death must happen to all persons. When the servant affirmed this, Siddhartha quickly realized the pointlessness of his luxurious life. For what is the point of pursuing pleasures that must always fade?

The fourth sight changed everything. Seeing the wandering holy man, poor and wearing only rags, but glowing radiantly with an inner wealth, Siddhartha realized that the spiritual life must be his path. Late one night he fled the palace, leaving behind his family and the only life he had ever known. Like Saint Francis, he cut off his hair and gave away his rich clothes. He sought out a well-known religious teacher and learned all he could, then moved on to another teacher, then another. He practiced extreme asceticism, fasting, meditating, and living a life of deprivation in the company of five other ascetic yogis.

After years of extreme self-mortification he had not found the answer to suffering. In his extremity a young girl offered him food and he accepted it. With new strength he saw that his intense asceticism was just as foolish as his former indulgence. He recognized that a middle way was better, avoiding both indulgence and deprivation. The myths tell us that through taking this path, Siddhartha quickly came to full understanding of this world and our experience of it. He sat down under a Bodhi tree and vowed not to move until he had attained enlightenment, no matter how long it took. He began to meditate. He looked deeply into his desires and his ignorance. Finally, seeing the morning star, his mind opened to reality: no separate Siddhartha really existed; his desires and his suffering vanished with the illusion of his self. He was enlightened, awakened, liberated. Siddhartha had become the Buddha.

In his freedom, Buddha began to teach others to be free. His path was open to all and he devoted the remainder of his long life to leading us along it. Living with his first followers he developed a set of practical guidelines for working toward enlightenment and living in harmony with others. Together, Buddha and his followers blazed a spiritual path that still calls to us today.

We've talked so far about Buddha, the person, but there is another side to Buddha. If Buddha the person experienced awakening, we as persons can do the same. When we do, we share Buddha Mind with everyone who has shared it throughout space and time. We become Buddha.

So the Buddha is still alive; he lives in us when we live as he taught. This can happen in two ways: the inner way of experiencing the world as Buddha did, and the outer way of living in the world as Buddha did. When we share his thought we share his nature. When we share his action we embody the dharma. Both ways we become Buddha.

What Did Buddha Teach?

This book tells us what Buddha would do in the difficult situations of modern work. Therefore it teases out strands of Buddhist teaching that apply not only to the time of Buddha but to our own age. So we want to provide an idea of what Buddha taught, as near as we know it. We can't provide an introduction to the whole richness of Buddhist teachings; we don't have the space to even *name* them. We simply want to give you a little hint, one we hope you will take and follow.

Right after awakening, Buddha taught his first sutta or sermon. All Buddhists share and value the core teachings found in the suttas. In them we find ourselves, our predicament, and our hope. Let's start where Buddha started.

With his first teaching, Buddha set rolling the wheel of truth that frees beings from the endless circle of life and death. Though this sutta is only a couple of pages long, it lays the foundation for all Buddhism to come. In it, Buddha tells a few serious renunciants of his awakening. He tells them there are two extremes they should not go to. One is the extreme of indulgence. Of course this was the whole of Buddha's first twenty-five years and it never led to happiness. Then Buddha tells them not to go to the other extreme, that of self-denial or self-torture. So what is the right path? It is the Middle Path, or the Middle Way, the way of Buddhism.

What happens when we follow this Middle Path? Ah, that is the power and the beauty of Buddhism. Buddha gives us our answer in The Four Noble Truths.

Buddha often referred to himself as a doctor. The Four Noble Truths are his diagnosis and course of treatment for us. First, he tells us we're sick; this is the First Noble Truth, that of dukkha (suffering, dissatisfaction). Second he diagnoses the disease; this is the Second Noble Truth, the origin of dukkha. Third he tells us there is a cure; this is the Third Noble Truth, the end of dukkha. Finally he gives us a prescription for the medicine to end our suffering; this is the Fourth Noble Truth, The Eightfold Path.

Life as we experience it is full of pain, frustration, disappointment, and suffering. We want what we can't have, or can't keep. We see ourselves sicken and others die. We age and are parted from those we love. No force can stop any of this, and so we suffer. This is the first Noble Truth of Buddhism, the truth of dukkha.

Such experiences cause us suffering because we feel we are separate beings, each finally alone in his or her reality. Because we orient our lives around this sense of self, we become attached to it and to what gives it pleasure. We strive to satisfy our desires, but this is a losing battle; we fail constantly, and in the end we all will fail permanently. This is the Second Noble Truth, the truth of the origin of dukkha.

Some, who seem to read no farther than the Second Noble Truth, see Buddha's teachings as pessimistic and hopeless. How unfortunate! Did they not notice there were four truths? And the third is the greatest. Buddha has just been enlightened, awakened to the deeper and wider reality of life. This is the great insight he has had and the great freedom he gives us. He now tells the renunciants that this whole painful process of birth and death is founded on ignorance and desire. Our suffering follows from our ignorance of how things really are. In our ignorance we cling to the self, its desires, and the suffering that follows; but such a self does not truly exist, and thus we have no need to suffer. This is the Third Noble Truth, the truth of the ending of ignorance and liberation from suffering.

Finally, Buddha reveals the Fourth Noble Truth, simply that following the Eightfold Noble Path will take us to the end of ignorance and liberate us from suffering. That path will free us. To follow that path perfectly is to become a Buddha, oneself. This is the teaching of Buddha and the practice of Buddhism, simple and yet world-changing. As Buddha says, "It is the Eightfold Noble Path: right views, right intention, right speech, right action, right livelihood, right effort, right mindfulness, right concentration. This, O monks, is the middle path, which gives insight and wisdom, and leads to calm, to vision, to enlightenment, to nirvana."

Buddha walked this path and taught it to his followers. He is the first jewel of Buddhism. His words became the dharma, the ongoing teacher for us even now. That dharma is the second jewel of Buddhism. Finally, his followers have tried to learn and embody that dharma, to become Buddhas, themselves. Those who strive sincerely form the sangha, the community of those walking the path together, the third jewel of Buddhism.

We walk this path as Buddhists but also as people who simply wish to be free and good in this world. No need to cling to views. The path does not start with views and end with concentration. The path is before us all at once. The path invites practice all the time. The path has no beginning. The path does not end.

Welcome.

Key Buddhist Terms

Bodhisattva: Literally, "awakening being"; a person who works to achieve liberation with and for all living beings.

Buddha: An awakened being; the first of the Three Jewels of Buddhism.

Buddhadharma: The teachings of Buddha.

Buddha Nature: The inherent potential in all beings to become Buddhas; effectively synonymous with "Buddha Mind."

Compassion: Sympathy and love for all beings; one of the two principle Buddhist virtues. Compassion leads to the wish to free all beings from dukkha.

Dharma or Dhamma: Can mean several things, but usually means the truth, the word of the Buddha, the Buddha's teachings; the second of the Three Jewels of Buddhism.

Dukkha: Literally, "dissatisfaction"; the existential suffering caused by desires and attachments (we all have it as long as we cling to our selves).

Eightfold Noble Path: The basic Buddhist way of living (see Appendix B) synonymous with "Middle Path" or "Middle Way" which are both synonymous with "Buddhism."

Four Noble Truths: Buddha's first teachings after enlightenment: 1) we all have suffering and dissatisfaction; 2) this suffering and dissatisfaction is caused by ignorance, desire, and attachment; 3) this suffering and dissatisfaction can end; 4) suffering and dissatisfaction are ended through following the Buddhist path (see Appendix B).

Haiku: A seventeen syllable Japanese poetic form, strongly associated with Zen Buddhism.

Karma: The effects of our acting with our body, speech, and mind. These effects serve as the cause for future events, including rebirths. Good actions cause good rebirths; bad actions cause bad rebirths. Often used in the popular sense as "what goes around comes around" or "as you sow, so shall you reap."

Lama: An incarnation of a Tibetan spiritual teacher or guru; the highest is the Dalai Lama.

Mahayana: Literally, "The Greater Vehicle"; the form of Buddhism that tries to realize awakening in all beings; predominant in East Asia.

Nirvana or Nibbana: Liberation from samsara (rebirth in the universe).

Pure Land: The Buddha Land of Amida Buddha, in which enlightenment is easy to experience; millions of Buddhists pray to be reborn here.

Right Livelihood: One of the eight factors of the Noble Eightfold Path; work that does little or no harm to all living things; what we all need to strive to make our own jobs become.

Roshi: Japanese Zen teacher.

Samsara: This universe of repeated existence; the world where we must continuously be reborn, die, be reborn, die . . . .

Sangha: The spiritual community, our spiritual friends; sometimes used to mean monks and nuns only, sometimes to mean all followers on the path; the third of the Three Jewels of Buddhism.

Shakyamuni Buddha: Literally "The Sage of the Shakyas, the Awakened One"; Gautama Siddhartha of the Shakya clan, the historical Buddha.

Shunyata: Emptiness; the belief that all things are empty of inherent existence—they do not exist except in an endless web of relations.

Sutra or Sutta: An oral teaching of the Buddha, eventually written down and put into one of several collections.

Tao (pronounced "Dow," as in Dow Jones): Literally, "The Way"; a central concept of East Asian religion, including Buddhism. Taoists are those following Taoism, the religion flowing from this idea.

Theravada: Literally, "The Way of the Elders"; the form of Buddhism founded on the community of monks and nuns striving for awakening; predominant in South and Southeast Asia.

Three Jewels of Buddhism: Buddha, dharma, and sangha: all a person needs to rely on, or take refuge in, to reach awakening.

Wisdom: An understanding of things that goes beyond intellectual knowing; one of the two principle Buddhist virtues. Wisdom comes from seeing the world and ourselves as we really are (or aren't).

Zen Buddhism: Literally, "Meditation Buddhism"; the East Asian Buddhist tradition emphasizing the struggle to realize one's original nature; called Ch'an in China, Sōn in Korea, Tien in Vietnam, and Zen in Japan.

Resources on Buddhism

As with all things, our little book must come to its end, yet we wish to give you something more to go on. So here is a list we've compiled of sources that bring Buddhism to life for us and will help you move further along the path of enlightened work.

Resources on Buddhism

An introduction to the richness of the whole Buddhist tradition, *The Vision of Buddhism*, by Roger Corless, allows us to walk out onto the landscape of Buddhism without dividing it into neat, academic domains.

What the Buddha Taught, a classic by the Sri Lankan monk and scholar Walpola Sri Rahula, expresses something of both early Buddhism and the Theravada tradition. Doctrinally focused, but beautifully clear.

Buddhism Plain & Simple, by Steve Hagen, is a perfect primer for beginners. Engaging, interesting, and lucidly written, it gives the reader a good grounding in the basics of Buddha's teachings. We also recommend it to those more experienced on the path.

Taigen Daniel Leighton's *Bodhisattva Archetypes* brings Mahayana Buddhism to life through its traditional religious figures, but also through contemporary figures who embody Mahayana's highest spirit. A great book to help us live as the bodhisattvas who walk among us.

His Holiness, the Dalai Lama's many books, for example, *Ethics for the New Millennium*, introduce the spirituality of Vajrayana (or Tibetan) Buddhism, as well as engage the larger sweep of world history and politics. You can even find many on audio cassettes.

For a practical introduction to Zen, including instructions on meditating, we suggest Robert Aitken Roshi's *Taking the Path of Zen*. Here, as in his other books, Aitken Roshi illuminates our lives with his magisterial yet supple blend of wisdom and compassion.

Being Black, by Angel Kyodo Williams, is a unique book, written with people of color in mind, yet remaining a resource for any reader. The author, a black, female Zen priest, combines an accessible writing style with valuable perspectives on Buddhism and real-life problems, both personal and professional.

What Book!?, an anthology of contemporary Buddha poems, assembled by Gary Gach, really speaks, chants, and sings to us. See what poems become part of your own path.

In this book we've given you many excerpts from the sacred texts of Buddhism, but we urge you to read more. A great many Theravada suttas are available on the World Wide Web at www.accesstoinsight.org; they even come with helpful introductions and commentaries. As for Mahayana Sutras, the Lotus Sutra, Vimalakirti Sutra, Diamond Sutra, and Heart Sutra remain vital and moving today and are available in many editions, anthologies, and the last three, online. Shantideva's Bodhicharyavatara (more properly spelled Bodhicāryavātra) charmingly brings the central teachings of Mahayana and Vajrayana Buddhism to life; let it inspire you as it has the Dalai Lama. Finally, try plunging into *The Roaring Stream*, a Zen reader edited by Nelson Foster and Jack Shoemaker, and into Kazuaki Tanahashi's two collections of the writings of Dogen, *Moon in a Dewdrop*, and *Enlightenment Unfolds*.

Buddhism is perhaps the best (not most, but best) represented of all religions online. We've mentioned where to find suttas. An excellent starting place for exploring contemporary Buddhism is www.dharmanet.org. From there you can go just about anywhere in Buddhist cyberspace.

Resources for Buddhism and Work

Building a Business the Buddhist Way, by Geri Larkin, we particularly recommend for entrepreneurs, small business owners, and those contemplating starting their own businesses. Wonderfully practical, with worksheets, and assignments, the book is part workbook, part textbook for the business owner or manager.

Zen and the Art of Making a Living, by Laurence G. Boldt, is the most comprehensive career resource for anyone seeking Right Livelihood. Not much Zen, but almost 600 pages chock-full of exercises, practical worksheets, how-to tips, and resources for making a life while making a living.

Work as a Spiritual Practice, by Lewis Richmond, explores conflict, stagnation, inspiration, accomplishment, and transformation of both the individual and the workplace, from a Zen perspective. *Zen at Work*, by Les Kaye, is a first-person story of a business executive who spent 30 years at IBM, while becoming a Zen teacher at the same time. Both of these are useful reading for anyone looking for role models in integrating spiritual practice with a real-world business career.

Enlightened Management, by Dona Witten with Akong Tulku Rinpoche, draws on *The Seven Points of Mind Training*. *The Diamond Cutter*, by Geshe Michael Roach, draws on *The Diamond Sutra*. Both books orient management practices to traditional values and practices in Tibetan Buddhism.

Franz Metcalf

Both Franz's background and his varied professional achievements combine the spiritual and the scholarly, religious feeling, and critical thinking. He began his graduate studies of religion fifteen years ago, getting his masters degree at Berkeley's Graduate Theological Union, comparing Buddhist and Christian spiritual practices. He earned a doctoral fellowship at the University of Chicago and continued his training, pursuing his abiding personal interest in Zen by writing his dissertation on the question, "Why do Americans practice Zen Buddhism?" He was awarded distinction on both his doctoral exams and his dissertation, receiving his Ph.D. in 1997.

In the ivory tower, Franz is co-chair of the Person, Culture, and Religion Group of the American Academy of Religion and has both led sessions and delivered papers at national scholarly meetings. He has published various articles and chapters and is Book Review Editor of the online *Journal of Global Buddhism*. Franz teaches religion at California State University, Los Angeles.

In the real world, Franz is among the national leaders of and edits the newsletter of the Forge Institute for Spirituality and Social Change, an organization devoted to interreligious dialogue and the creation of a more spiritually centered society. Franz is also the author of *What Would Buddha Do?: 101 Answers to Life's Daily Dilemmas* (Berkeley: Seastone, 1999), the prequel to this book, a bestseller distributed in six languages. He continues to inquire into Buddhism and psychology, in America and in his own life.

You can contact Franz at franzmetcalf@earthlink.net. For seminars, keynote speeches, and workshops, you can reach both Franz and BJ at their Web site: www.buddhaatwork.com.

BJ Gallagher Hateley

BJ sees her work as a spiritual calling. She preaches the gospel of humanistic management, helping her clients create a kinder, gentler workplace.

BJ has built her business on the success of her international bestseller, *A Peacock in the Land of Penguins* (12 languages; 150,000 copies), as well as her other books, *Customer at the Crossroads*, *Pigeonholed in the Land of Penguins* and *Is It Always Right to be Right?* She also develops assessment tools, and writes and produces animated training videos.

Among BJ's clients are corporations, professional associations, nonprofit groups, and government agencies, including DaimlerChrysler, IBM, Chevron, Kellogg, Toyota, Planned Parenthood, Volkswagen, Phoenix Newspapers, Inc., and the City of Pasadena. She has conducted seminars and delivered keynotes in Latin America, Canada, and Europe.

BJ is a Phi Beta Kappa graduate of the University of Southern California, where she also pursued (but never caught) a Ph.D. in Social Ethics. Her first book, *Telling Your Story, Exploring Your Faith*, was written while she was the Director of Staff Development at USC. She then moved on to serve as Training Manager for the *Los Angeles Times*.

In writing *What Would Buddha Do at Work?* BJ has come full circle, integrating her interest in spirituality with her business background.

You can reach BJ at Peacock Productions, 701 Danforth Drive, Los Angeles, CA 90065. Phone: 323-227-6205. Fax: 323-227-0705. E-mail: bbjjgallagher@aol.com. For seminars, keynote speeches and workshops, you can reach Franz and BJ at their Web site: www.buddhaatwork.com.

For Your Free
W.W.B.D.@W. Bracelet

Seastone / Ulysses Press and Berrett-Koehler would like to invite you to wear a "What Would Buddha Do at Work?" ("W.W.B.D.@W.") bracelet.

The idea is simple but powerful: wear your W.W.B.D.@W. bracelet to remind yourself—like a string around your finger—to stop before acting and ask yourself, "What would Buddha do in my current situation?"

To receive your free bracelet, send your name and address along with your receipt showing proof of purchase of this book to:

Free W.W.B.D.@W. Bracelet

Seastone / Ulysses Press

P.O. Box 3440

Berkeley, CA 94703

(Additional W.W.B.D.@W. bracelets may be purchased from Ulysses Press for $3.00 each.)